OECD
ECONOMIC
SURVEYS

2000-2001

Austria

OECD

ORGANISATION FOR ECONOMIC CO-OPERATION AND DEVELOPMENT

ORGANISATION FOR ECONOMIC CO-OPERATION AND DEVELOPMENT

Pursuant to Article 1 of the Convention signed in Paris on 14th December 1960, and which came into force on 30th September 1961, the Organisation for Economic Co-operation and Development (OECD) shall promote policies designed:

- to achieve the highest sustainable economic growth and employment and a rising standard of living in Member countries, while maintaining financial stability, and thus to contribute to the development of the world economy;

- to contribute to sound economic expansion in Member as well as non-member countries in the process of economic development; and

- to contribute to the expansion of world trade on a multilateral, non-discriminatory basis in accordance with international obligations.

The original Member countries of the OECD are Austria, Belgium, Canada, Denmark, France, Germany, Greece, Iceland, Ireland, Italy, Luxembourg, the Netherlands, Norway, Portugal, Spain, Sweden, Switzerland, Turkey, the United Kingdom and the United States. The following countries became Members subsequently through accession at the dates indicated hereafter: Japan (28th April 1964), Finland (28th January 1969), Australia (7th June 1971), New Zealand (29th May 1973), Mexico (18th May 1994), the Czech Republic (21st December 1995), Hungary (7th May 1996), Poland (22nd November 1996), Korea (12th December 1996) and the Slovak Republic (14th December 2000). The Commission of the European Communities takes part in the work of the OECD (Article 13 of the OECD Convention).

Publié également en français.

Table of contents

Boxes

Tables

Figures

BASIC STATISTICS OF AUSTRIA, 2000

THE LAND

Area (1 000 sq. km)	84	Major cities	
Agricultural area (1 000 sq. km)	34	(thousand of inhabitants)	
Exploited forest area (1 000 sq. km)	33	Vienna	1 608
		Graz	241
		Linz	188
		Salzburg	144
		Innsbruck	112

THE PEOPLE

Population (thousands)	8 107	Net migration, 1999 thousands	20
Number of inhabitans per sq. km	97	Total employment[1] thousands	4 046
Net natural increase, 1999 thousands	0	*of which*: Primary sector	543
Net natural increase per		Secondary sector	1014
1 000 inhabitants, 1999	0	Tertiary sector	2 489

PRODUCTION

Gross domestic product (Sch billion)	2 819	Industrial origin of GDP at market prices	
Per head, US$	23 286	(per cent)	
Gross fixed capital formation	668	Agriculture	1.8
Per cent of GDP	24	Industry	22.5
Per head US$	5 515	Construction	7.8
		Other	67.8

THE GOVERNMENT

Per cent of GDP		Composition of federal Parliament	
Public consumption	19.4	Socialist Party	65
General government current revenue	51.1	Austrian People's Party	52
General government net lending	−1.1	Freedom Union	52
		Liberal Forum	−
		Greens	14
		Last general election : December 1999	

FOREIGN TRADE

Exports of goods and services		Imports of goods and services	
as a per cent of GDP	50.1	as a per cent of GDP	51.1
Main exports (per cent of merchandise		Main imports (per cent of merchandise	
exports) :		imports) :	
Food, beverage, tobacco	4.6	Food, beverage, tobacco	5.0
Raw materials and energy	4.7	Raw materials and energy	10.4
Semi-finished goods	14.5	Semi-finished goods	12.8
Finished goods	76.2	Finished goods	71.7
of which: Consumer goods	49.0	*of which*: Consumer goods	46.2

THE CURRENCY

Irrevocable conversion rate (€1)	13.7603	Currency units of euro per US$, average of	
		daily figures :	
		Year 2000	1.0851
		October 2001	1.1038

1.   Domestic concept.

Note: An international comparison of certain basic statistics is given in an Annex table.

This Survey is published on the responsibility of the Economic and Development Review Committee of the OECD, which is charged with the examination of the economic situation of Member countries.

●

The economic situation and policies of Austria were reviewed by the Committee on 25 September 2001. The draft report was then revised in the light of the discussions and given final approval as the agreed report by the whole Committee on 26 November 2001.

●

The Secretariat's draft report was prepared for the Committee by Eckhard Wurzel and Jens Høj under the supervision of Andreas Wörgötter.

●

The previous Survey of Austria was issued in May 1999.

Assessment and recommendations

A well performing economy that could do better

Economic growth in Austria since the mid-1990s has been roughly in line with the EU average. However, it appears that the economy has not yet embarked on a path of higher trend growth even though Austria's EU accession in 1995 and the market transition of eastern European countries eliminated many entry barriers for Austrian exporters and importers. While trade shares increased rapidly, Austria lost market share. Two broad issues deserve special attention with respect to raising Austria's growth potential. Firstly budgetary consolidation was delayed for too long, and a distortionary fiscal stop-and-go policy adopted. In a similar vein, significant public sector reform was delayed in the 1990s, precluding the potentially positive impact of such reform on the functioning of the economy overall. Secondly, Austria delayed reform of its regulatory framework. This is understandable, since this framework successfully supported high economic growth during earlier times of relatively modest structural change. However, reaping positive growth effects from increased international integration and more rapid technological change requires more thorough reform in product and labour markets favouring market determined outcomes and higher structural flexibility. Ongoing policy action is already proceeding along these lines, but the remaining challenges of overdue structural reform are significant. While the first chapter reviews the main macroeconomic forces at work and the Secretariat's projections, issues of fiscal policy and structural reform are highlighted in Chapters II and III of this report. Finally, Chapter IV considers in some detail issues associated with encouraging environmentally sustainable economic development.

*External
developments
dominated
the business cycle
over the last
two years...*

Real GDP growth in 2000 totalled 3.0 per cent, well above potential, and in line with the average in the EU. The Austrian economy participated in the economic upswing within the EU that was driven by accelerating world trade in the second half of 1999 and into 2000. On the domestic side, the upswing was underpinned by strong private consumption, with disposable incomes benefiting from tax cuts that became effective in January 2000, and robust growth in investment in machinery and equipment. But the economy's momentum slowed in the second half of 2000 and into 2001 as world trade growth decelerated. Private consumption growth declined as consumer price inflation increased, mainly due to higher oil prices and the weakening of the exchange rate. Investment in machinery and equipment also grew at a slower pace from the second half of 2000 on, while construction investment was weak throughout. Employment continued to grow, but at a decelerating rate with unemployment even increasing in recent months. Consumer price inflation peaked in spring 2001, at a rate of 3¼ per cent. Higher indirect taxes added to the increase in the price level. But by mid-2001, inflation had come down substantially, as the effects of the previous oil and import price increases began petering out, and the impact of last year's indirect tax increases levelled off. While wages picked up in 2000, wage settlements remained moderate, supporting employment generation.

*... slowing growth
temporarily
this year and next,
though activity
is projected
to pick up from
the second half
of next year on*

Growth in 2001 is likely to be markedly lower than the year before, dropping to a rate significantly below potential in the OECD's projections. This reflects the deceleration in world trade and slowing domestic demand that have been evident during the course of the year, and this weakness is now reinforced by the negative global growth shock emanating from the 11 September terrorist attack on the United States. Adverse confidence effects of this event are projected to weaken global activity and trade well into the first half next year. But world trade growth may begin to strengthen again thereafter, leading to a progressive pick-up in Austrian activity which will also be supported by more vigorous domestic demand. Indeed, private consumption is likely to recover as consumer confidence stabilises, driven by rising disposable incomes, rises in family benefits and improving terms of trade. Investment in machinery and equipment should also gather momentum, following the improvement in external demand. Construction will remain subdued in 2002 but should strengthen thereafter. While government consumption is projected to slow, owing to ongoing fiscal consolidation, monetary conditions are projected to support growth. All in all, GDP growth is projected to rebound in the second half of next year and to accelerate further in 2003, allowing the output gap, that is opening in 2001 and 2002, to begin to close again. Risks to these projections consist mainly in a slower-than-expected recovery in world trade which could, in particular, postpone the projected upswing in Germany, Austria's main trading partner.

General government balances improved slowly...

Fiscal consolidation was essentially put on hold after 1997, so that the general government deficit widened in 1998 and was roughly unchanged in 1999. In 2000 implementation of the federal budget was delayed due to the transition phase associated with establishing the new government after the general elections; and tax cuts and phased increases in family benefits that became effective in January 2000 further complicated the task of returning to a consolidation track. Nevertheless, in 2000 the general government deficit was reduced by 1 percentage point of GDP, to 1.1 per cent, mainly as the result of higher annual growth, one-off receipts from the auctioning of UMTS mobile phone licenses – totalling 0.4 per cent of GDP – as well as revenue-raising measures installed by the new administration.

... with plans to consolidate further this year and next

The government aimed in the 2000 Stability Programme to reduce the general government deficit to ¾ per cent of GDP in 2001, balance the budget by 2002, and maintain balance thereafter. To this end a consolidation programme has been put forward consisting of both expenditure restraint and revenue raising measures. On the expenditure side, savings are to be generated largely by structural reform measures, notably pension reform, reductions in government employment on the federal and the local level, more focused targeting in the provision of social transfers, and measures designed to slim down the public administration and transferring tasks to the public enterprise sector. Some initiatives along these lines have already been implemented while others still need to be decided. On the revenue side, some measures to broaden the tax base have been taken, but a significant part of the consolidation in 2001 consists of one-off measures. Higher than expected business tax instalments and lower interest payments in late 2001 imply that a balanced budget is likely to be reached already this year. On the other hand, the sharp deceleration in economic activity has made it considerably more difficult to maintain balance in 2002. The Secretariat projects for 2002, assuming both the implementation of the budgeted consolidation measures and scheduled increases in child benefits, a deficit of almost ½ per cent of GDP, reflecting essentially the budgetary effect of the automatic stabilisers.

Structural reform and strict spending control are needed to make the fiscal turn-around sustainable

Earlier episodes of fiscal consolidation in Austria in the last decade were succeeded by rapidly rising structural deficits. This reflects both the fact that past consolidation policies relied to a large extent on one-off measures and also that, with fiscal balances improving, new social entitlement programmes were instituted. In the present phase, balancing the budget over a couple of years appears feasible even though growth has slowed. However, several risks, both on the revenue and on the spending side, require tight spending control for the medium-term consolidation targets to be met. Most importantly, one-off measures play a significant role in the government's savings programme, and not all parts of envisaged structural reform have yet been decided or implemented. Moreover, new spending programmes are envisaged, with the new family benefits that will come into effect in January 2002 placing a heavy burden on the general government budget, accounting for some ⅓ per cent of GDP. Hence, a sustainable elimination of the general government deficit requires rapid replacement of the one-off measures by structural policies that are associated with lasting savings. The government should identify spending programmes where cuts can be made. Over the next years tax reductions should be implemented, but have to be backed up by structural reductions in government spending. Otherwise, there is a risk of a renewed spending cycle that would endanger the achievements made. Moreover, creating a budgetary surplus would help cope with fiscal pressures associated with ageing.

Public sector reform should be deeply rooted and implemented quickly...

Reforming various aspects of the public sector ranks high on the government's policy agenda. Indeed, public sector reform is important both for fiscal consolidation and for increasing the sector's efficiency and widening the scope of market-determined outcomes. While some elements of the reform have been decided, notably the reduction of public sector employment and the streamlining of some parts of public sector administration, important elements are outstanding. Taking tasks out of the government sector and incorporating them in the public enterprise sector, as scheduled, can increase public sector efficiency under certain conditions. However, the evidence from previous action yields a mixed picture, and there is even the risk that spinning off companies from the budget might reduce fiscal discipline. Thus, such action can be no substitute for fundamental reform. Effective duplication within public sector administrations should be identified and abolished. Moreover, choices need to be made as to what services should be left to the private sector for provision; action in this field can be based on proposals that have already been made by a reform commission – the *Aufgabenreformkommission*. Analysis of the costs and benefits of policies needs to be developed, and for this purpose a coherent framework for *ex ante* and *ex post* project evaluation needs to be established. Efficient project selection requires estimating the likely future revenues and expenditures over a horizon of several decades and assessing their present value.

... and the congruence of spending and revenue raising powers at the various levels of government should be improved

Issues of public sector efficiency also arise with respect to the allocation of tasks and revenue raising powers across the different levels of government. The process of negotiating revenue sharing is non-transparent and the system provides few incentives at sub-central levels of government for efficient use of resources and for evaluating the efficiency of spending plans. Instead, general tax receipts should be distributed across government levels in accordance with fixed principles, and the revenue raising powers of the *Länder* and communities should be exercised and extended if necessary. In the same vein, ongoing policy initiatives aiming to improve the assignment of tasks by government level should focus on increasing the congruence between spending and financing responsibilities.

Fundamental pension reform is necessary

Important steps were taken in 2000 to limit the fiscal impact of ageing on the public pay-as-you-go system, in particular by making early retirement less attractive. Pre-empting the rapid rise of pension claims over the next years and decades requires further reform however, which should be implemented soon. Increasing retirement ages appears particularly important, and further reform in this field would have to consider all potential channels into early retirement, including invalidity pensions. Also, the fragmentation of the pension system into different occupational branches, each serving its own clientele, should be abolished. To strengthen the link between pension contributions and pensions received, entitlements should be related to the retirees' earnings base during their entire work history rather than the best 15 years. The redistributive role of the system should be identified and redistribution should be financed out of general taxes instead of wage-based contributions. Benefits provided by the pay-as-you-go part of the system should be adjusted so as to secure the system's fiscal sustainability, and a supplementary funded layer should be developed. This could be achieved by transforming the system of severance pay into compulsory company-based funded pensions. Already existing private pension investment funds have hardly been accepted yet by households, despite preferential tax treatment. The evolution of such funds should therefore be monitored, and the regulatory framework reconsidered if necessary.

Measures have been taken to reduce non-wage labour costs and raise incentives for job search, leaving scope for further improvement

The Austrian labour market continues to exhibit a comparatively low level of unemployment and a high degree of aggregate wage flexibility. The relatively moderate wage increases and steady employment growth seen in 2000, at a time of significant oil and import price hikes, validate this finding. But labour utilisation of females and older workers is low, and there is a mismatch developing between qualifications demanded and supplied. With respect to labour market reform, the new government is emphasising the need to increase incentives in the labour market and the effectiveness of job placement, and significant policy initiatives along these lines have either been implemented or are in preparation. Some eligibility rules for receiving unemployment benefits have been tightened and this should strengthen the incentives for job search. Measures to reduce non-wage labour costs and improve the targeting of social transfers have also been taken. Scope for further action remains, however, and not all measures taken appear to be consistent with raising incentives for labour force participation and employment creation. Indeed, this is likely to be true for subsidies extended for working time reductions of older employees (*Altersteilzeit*), which need to be reconsidered. Also, the extension of child benefits scheduled for 2002 is likely on balance to reduce working hours supplied by parents, particularly women. In the unemployment insurance, the lengthening of the period of unemployment benefit receipt is likely to adversely affect job search and should be revised. Plans to widen the definition of "acceptable jobs" with respect to the skill profiles for recipients of unemployment related benefits should be implemented, and the acceptability criteria should be progressively broadened with unemployment duration.

Better job placement would improve labour market outcomes

A key aspect of the envisaged reform of the Public Employment Service (PES) is achieving a better integration of the PES activities concerning counselling, job placement, provision of active labour market measures and provision of unemployment benefits. Indeed, the efficiency of the job matching process has been found elsewhere to increase with the interaction between the different functions in the placement process, and initiatives to better integrate these functions are therefore welcome. Similarly, better integrating the unemployment assistance and social assistance systems, for which responsibilities are dispersed between the federal and the regional authorities, needs to be considered. Moreover, the scope for private placement agencies within an integrated employment service should be widened. Active labour market policies (ALMPs) play an important role in the government's employment strategy. Within a framework of improving the "profiling" of the unemployed with respect to relevant economic characteristics, ALMPs should be better utilised to test the readiness of benefit recipients to take up work. Moreover, to secure the effectiveness of training and work provision schemes, measures should be tightly targeted on problem groups. In general, there is a risk that private sector entrepreneurial activity is crowded out by public work programmes, and associated deadweight costs are often substantial. Appropriate evaluation of the effectiveness of the measures utilised with respect to increasing employment chances and minimising dead weight cost and crowding out effects is therefore imperative and should be stepped up. Putting more emphasis on in-work benefits that ease marginal effective taxation associated with the transition into regular employment can be a promising strategy for "activating" unemployment-related benefits and social assistance schemes.

Reform of the education system is being addressed and should rank high on the policy agenda

The increasing importance of skilled human capital in a "knowledge-based society" reinforces the need for reforming Austria's education system. Tertiary education in Austria has been found costly and its allocational efficiency needs to be improved to cope with a widening gap in skills provided and demanded. The government has embarked on a reform programme aiming at raising the quality of tertiary education and the efficiency of university funding. Major elements of the programme are the abolition of lifelong tenure for university teachers, the introduction of performance-related elements both into the remuneration system for teachers and the funding of the universities more generally, and a higher degree of university autonomy in designing their areas of research and education. From autumn 2001 onwards, students will be charged tuition fees, the proceeds of which will be redistributed to the universities. The plans for university reform go in the right direction and should be carried through. In particular, while the introduction of tuition fees is welcome, raising the financial endowment of the universities is not sufficient for improving performance. Rather, reform should quickly move on to establishing a higher degree of competition between universities and a link between the universities' performance and their funding. Austria's dual apprenticeship system has been successful hitherto in providing applied skills, thereby contributing to holding down youth unemployment to comparatively low levels. Efforts have been made over the past years to adapt apprenticeship curricula to new demands. This policy needs to continue. Markets should be allowed to adjust pay scales so as to balance demands and supply for training across occupations.

Forthcoming competition legislation should strengthen enforceability

The current regulatory system for general competition issues – particularly mergers and cartels – is based on a cartel court that has limited legal powers to instigate actions independently, but acts on the recommendations of the social partners, with the Minister of Economic Affairs and Labour representing the state before the court. The government has tabled legislation to establish an independent competition authority, and this would mark important progress towards a system of effective competition enforcement. To secure effectiveness the institutional design needs to be streamlined. Firms violating the law should be subject to fines set sufficiently high to deter anti-competitive activity (particularly cartels). Adopting a leniency programme should be considered whereby the first firm to divulge the existence of a cartel and to co-operate fully in its prosecution would be eligible for reduced sanctions. Also, it needs to be established whether personnel are sufficient to secure effective investigation, with staffing being increased quickly if necessary.

Regulatory reform of network industries is progressing, but open issues remain

There have been some positive developments in network industries, and significant steps have been made to open some markets to competition. Prevailing market structures suggest however, that a lot remains to be done to firmly establish competition in network industries. As in almost all OECD countries, regulatory reform in telecommunication led to sizeable price cuts and a widening range of services. Partial market opening has also induced price cuts for electricity. In the electricity and the gas sectors the government has scheduled full market opening for fall 2001 and 2002, respectively, well ahead of the requirements stipulated in the respective EU directives, but this needs to be backed up by further reform. Regulatory reform in the postal sector, on the other hand, is not particularly advanced, and little progress has been made with respect to introducing competition in the railways system. Policy action in these fields could be expected to generate potentially very substantial welfare improvements for consumers and to contribute to increasing productivity growth in the economy. Major open issues are:

- In *telecommunication* the regulatory framework should be extended so as to allow pro-active measures, that follow rapidly changing market structures, of the telecommunication regulator on its own initiative. To increase competitive pressures in the mobile phone market number portability should be imposed.

– With vertically-integrated utilities dominating *electricity and gas markets*, effective non-discriminatory access to networks is not fully secured. Thus, to strengthen competition, grids need to be completely unbundled from distribution and generation. At the minimum, this requires a separation of networks and generators into different legal entities. This should be reinforced by privatising utilities.

– In the *postal sector* the Austrian Post has exclusive rights for delivery of letters weighing up to 350 grams. This monopoly right should be reduced and preferably terminated. The regulatory competence should be transferred from the Ministry of Transport, Innovation and Technology to a strong independent regulator.

– In the *railway sector* entry of private providers of transportation services should be fostered. This requires, in particular, that independence be established of the grid from the provider of transport services.

Important regulatory issues also arise with respect to non-network sectors. The regulation of shop opening hours should be liberalised further. Public procurement rules should be made uniform across the different layers of government, based on open tendering. Privatisation should be extended to the remaining state-owned banks at all levels of government.

Environmental standards are high in Austria, but the policy framework needs to be improved

Environmental standards are high in Austria, and this is reflected in elaborate environmental regulations, the incorporation of environmental concerns in the planning of major infrastructure projects and Austria's ambitious international commitments. Environmental objectives are backed by a very broad political consensus, and substantial financial resources are devoted to meeting environmental goals. However, a well-established framework for integrating environmental concerns into general policy planning is lacking. In particular, there is little *ex ante* and *ex post* evaluation of implied economic costs and potential environmental benefits. Not least, this implies that policies directed at similar objectives are not well balanced so as to secure high degrees of overall efficiency. A consistent framework for cost-benefit analysis across policies should therefore be introduced.

An ambitious Kyoto target serves as the flagship of Austria's climate change policy

A prime example for Austria's ambitious environmental goals are large reductions of greenhouse gas emissions. However, the policy mix applied for this purpose can be improved. While much emphasis is put on "command-and-control" type regulations, economic instruments are not closely linked to environmental goals: taxes on energy provide little incentives for more environmentally-friendly economic behaviour and certain subsidies are given without sufficient evaluation. In particular, effectiveness of current regulation concerning the efficiency of motors and heating plants could be enhanced by the introduction of a CO_2 tax or trading scheme. Thereby emission reduction would become a matter of economic self-interest, reducing the need for costly technical controls. The CO_2 tax would allow to better focus the structure of energy taxes on the abatement of greenhouse gas emissions. Exemptions that are not environmentally motivated – such as preferential taxation of diesel – should be abolished. A CO_2 tax could also reduce the need for environmentally motivated subsidy programmes aiming at supporting renewable energy sources, thermal insulation of the existing housing stock, central heating plants and public transport. Social concerns could be addressed via means-tested social transfers. Moreover, concerns about negative impacts on Austria's international competitiveness could be dealt with via a grandfathering scheme that maintains incentives for new investment.

Road pricing that generates incentives to avoid environmentally damaging traffic should replace the eco-point system

NO_x emissions associated with transit traffic of trucks were successfully reduced via an eco-point system, negotiated along with Austria's EU-accession, in which NO_x-related points are allocated to trucks. It is unlikely, however that the transit agreement can be indefinitely extended. Moreover, the present system provides insufficient incentives to utilise clean transport technologies in trucks. Thus, the regulation of transit traffic needs to rely on increasing the marginal cost of environmentally damaging transit to replace the present "eco-point" system, and this suggests introducing a road pricing system that takes into account the environmental costs of transportation through sensitive regions. The pertinent EU legislation should be adjusted accordingly in the light of the recently published EU White Paper.

Introducing full cost recovery pricing while phasing out capital cost subsidies could secure water service infrastructure investments for the future

Water issues are considered with high priority by the Austrian public, hence the Austrian government aims at making sure that sufficient investments in water service infrastructure are made in order to maintain the high quality of water. Improved efficiency in achieving this objective could be promoted by phasing down capital cost subsidies for water treatment while moving in parallel towards full cost recovery pricing principles, thus revealing particularly inefficient water service providers, increasing the efficiency of the water service infrastructure and improving resource allocation. This would fully support the envisaged and the already implemented measures as stipulated in the Austrian government programme. Also, waste collection and treatment charges should be set as to reflect the costs of emissions into air and soil. Such a system could improve efficiency in the disposal of waste.

Environmental services from agriculture should be exposed to cost-benefit analysis

In agriculture many efforts were made to promote more environmentally friendly practices. However, resource allocation could be improved if the support system were changed from being production method oriented to be targeted at specific environmental outcomes via cost-benefit analysis. This would be enhanced by cost sharing with tourism, to the extent tourism benefits from the landscape preservation due to farming. The current excess supply of certain organically farmed output suggests that more room should be provided for market determined outcomes while administrative measures should focus on framework conditions.

Summing up

Economic growth in Austria is currently weakening and will be adversely affected by the global shock emanating from the 11 September terrorist attacks in the United States. However, growth is projected to recover from the second half of next year on, reflecting an expected improvement in world trade and monetary conditions that will not act as a brake on GDP growth. However, important challenges remain if Austria is to raise its growth potential and fully benefit from European integration. Wide-ranging structural reforms announced by the government include putting the pension system on a fiscally sustainable base, increasing the efficiency of the public sector, tightening the targeting of social benefits, improving incentives in the labour market, opening network industries to competition, and lifting the performance of the education system. Most of these initiatives go in the right direction, and would accelerate the pace of structural reform if they were fully implemented. Several policy measures along these lines are already in force or being introduced. In some cases, however, policies appear to be at variance with improving economic incentives or fostering fiscal consolidation. It is particularly unfortunate in this respect that the government is introducing a major extension of an already generous child cash support system which is likely to exert a negative impact on working hours supplied by parents. More fundamental pension reform is necessary, the efficiency of job placement needs to be improved and plans for university reform should be carried out. While good progress has been made with respect to competition legislation, market opening needs to be backed up by further reform. A sustainable elimination of the general government deficit requires rapid replacement of budgeted one-off measures by structural policies that are associated with lasting savings. For this purpose spending programmes should be identified that can be cut. More efficient project selection also requires establishing an effective framework of *ex ante* and *ex post* policy cost evaluation. Effective duplication within public-sector administrations should be identified and abolished, and choices need to be made as to what services should be left to the private sector for provision. While eliminating the general government deficit should remain the primary short-term consolidation target, creating a general government surplus in the medium-term would help cope with fiscal pressure associated with population ageing. As regards environmentally-sustainable growth, Austria is acting from a position of relatively good environmental performance and with the ambition to further improve environmental outcomes. However, the policy mix being used relies too much on command-

and-control type measures, while economic instruments – both in the form of subsidies and taxes – are not linked tightly enough to environmental goals, resulting in higher costs and distortions. Thus, more use should be made of economic instruments to improve environmental performance notably, by introducing a CO_2 tax. Moreover, an integrated approach is needed that systematically utilises cost-benefit analysis and *ex post* programme evaluations to formulate environmental policies and reduce the economic burden of reaching environmental targets. Progress on all these scores is essential to facilitate the necessary institutional changes allowing Austria to further improve living standards, support social cohesion and maintain an attractive environment.

I. Austria in line with the international business cycle

Overview

Economic activity recovered in the course of 1999 as private consumption was boosted by a family package phased in over the year and exports accelerated in line with a strong expansion of world trade. Economic growth strengthened further in 2000 totalling 3 per cent for the year as a whole, and widening further the positive output gap that had emerged earlier. However, the economy's momentum slowed in the second half of the year as foreign trade decelerated following the abrupt slowdown of the US economic expansion. Moreover, private consumption growth moderated during the year, as consumer price inflation increased – partly as a result of rising oil and other import prices, but also revenue raising fiscal measures – reducing real income growth. Import growth weakened somewhat but remained fairly robust and the current account deficit stabilised at relatively high levels. Thus, by the end of 2000 the economy grew at a pace below that of the Secretariat's estimate of potential growth. It slowed much further in the first half of 2001. Despite the slowing of economic activity, unemployment – already lower than in most other EU countries – fell in early 2001 to its lowest rate in a decade, before it slowly increased. Consumer price inflation has declined since spring 2001 with oil prices dropping.

Economic indicators coming in since mid-2001 are pointing to a further deterioration of activity. Both the business and the consumer confidence declined further, and these developments are being reinforced by the negative consequences on confidence, domestically and internationally, emanating from the 11 September terrorist attacks in the United States. Nevertheless, private consumption can be expected to remain the main source of growth in the remainder of 2001. Public consumption is being curbed by a fiscal consolidation programme aiming to eliminate the general government deficit by 2002 and investment is being held back by declining growth in foreign and domestic demand and low capacity utilisation. Activity is expected to remain weak well into the first half of 2002, when the external sector is expected to benefit from the projected recovery in world trade, which eventually translates into higher incomes and thus stronger private domestic demand.[1] Consumer price inflation is expected to come down further in line with lower oil prices and as the effects of last year's hike in indirect taxes disappear.

Since 1995 Austrian external trade has benefited from higher annual export market growth for goods amounting to 9 per cent as compared with less than 6 per cent in the preceding decade.[2] Similarly, Austrian foreign trade relative to GDP grew faster than that in the European average. This reflects the EU accession as well as the ongoing integration with Austria's eastern neighbours. Also, Austrian exporters managed to increase their export market shares in the second half of the 1990s. However, while Austria's economic activity picked up at the end of the 1990s, its growth performance has been trailing the developments in other European countries, and in particular the other 1995 accession countries (Figure 1). Indeed, large and persistent current account deficits since 1995 indicate an asymmetric effect of the increase in international economic integration (Figure 2, Panel D). While foreign suppliers apparently took advantage of easier access to the Austrian market, this was not matched by increases in Austrian exports of a similar size. Further efforts to improve the flexibility of the goods and labour markets are therefore important for increasing the competitiveness of Austrian producers in domestic and foreign markets, and allow Austria to reap the full benefits of international integration on economic growth. The origins of other European countries' product market reforms can at least be traced back to the start of EU's internal market programme, whereas similar reforms in Austria only began in earnest with the EU accession. The ongoing reform process is beneficial for enhancing competition and eventually growth, but the novelty of the deregulation programme implies that the benefits from the reforms still have to materialise. Thus, competitive product and labour markets will prepare Austria for future international challenges and opportunities, pointing to the benefits of adapting a more pro-active policy stance in the ongoing regulatory reform programme.

The economy slowed during 2000

Growth became more reliant on domestic demand as exports faltered

The economy entered 2000 at a pace well above the Secretariat's estimate for its potential rate of growth, with private consumption being boosted by a non-financed tax reform raising disposable incomes, and exports benefiting from the continued strong growth in world trade (Figure 2). However, the economy's momentum weakened during 2000 and in the first half of 2001, bringing GDP growth below potential. While nominal disposable incomes were boosted by higher growth of wages and entrepreneurial incomes and income tax reductions, private consumption decelerated as consumer price inflation rose. The latter

Figure 1. **Real GDP growth and export and import shares**

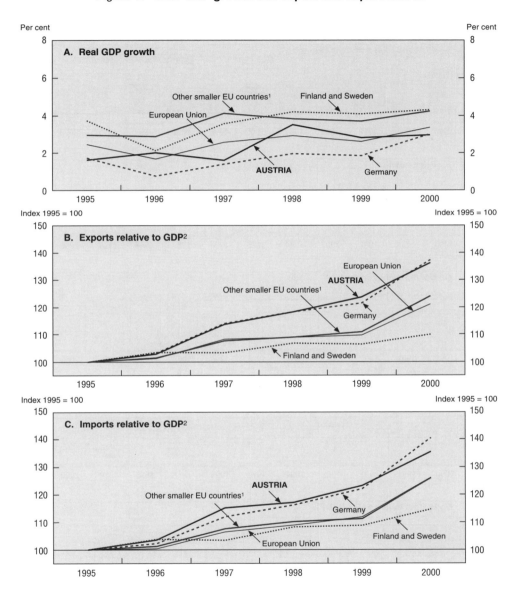

1. EU countries excluding Austria, Finland, France, Germany, Italy, Spain, Sweden and United Kingdom.
2. Balance of payments basis; exports and imports of goods and services.
Source: Austrian Institute for Economic Research (WIFO) and OECD, *Main Economic Indicators* and *National Accounts*.

Figure 2.   **Macroeconomic performance**
Per cent

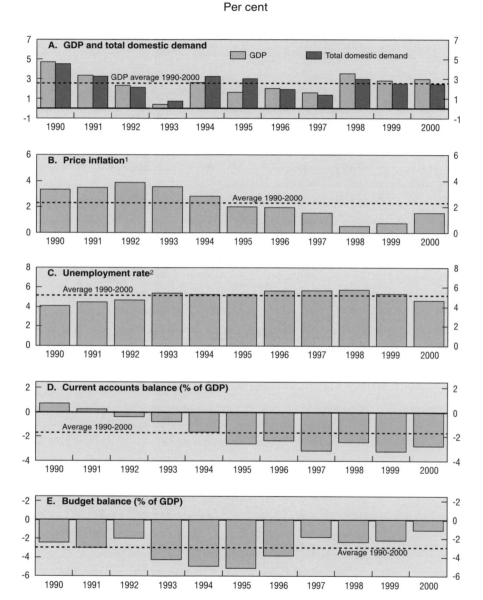

1. Private consumption deflator.
2. Registered unemployment as a percentage of total labour force, including self-employment.
Source: OECD.

Table 1. **Demand and output**

Percentage change from previous year, constant 1995 prices

	1984-94 average	1995	1996	1997	1998	1999	2000	2001SI year-on-year
Private consumption	2.8	2.6	3.2	1.7	2.8	2.7	2.5	1.4
Government consumption	2.2	1.3	1.2	−1.5	2.8	2.2	0.9	−1.1
Gross fixed investment	4.1	1.3	2.2	2.0	3.4	1.5	5.1	0.5
Construction	4.2	0.5	0.3	−1.0	1.3	−0.7	0.3	−1.3
Machinery and equipment	4.0	2.4	5.1	6.5	6.4	4.3	11.1	2.3
Changes in stock[1]	0.0	0.6	−0.6	0.5	−0.2	0.5	−0.3	0.2
Total domestic demand	2.8	2.6	1.9	1.6	2.7	2.8	2.5	0.9
Exports of goods and services	4.6	3.0	5.2	12.4	7.9	8.7	12.2	7.7
of which: Goods[2]	4.9	12.0	4.5	16.3	8.2	7.9	13.5	6.6
Imports of goods and services	4.8	5.6	4.9	12.0	5.9	8.8	11.1	6.3
of which: Goods[2]	5.1	6.1	4.4	9.8	7.6	7.2	10.8	8.3
Foreign balance[1]	−0.1	−0.9	0.1	0.0	0.8	0.0	0.5	0.8
Gross domestic product	2.7	1.6	2.0	1.6	3.5	2.8	3.0	1.7
Memorandum items:								
GDP deflator	2.9	2.5	1.3	0.9	0.5	0.7	1.2	2.1
Private consumption deflator	2.7	2.0	1.9	1.5	0.5	0.7	1.5	2.3
Unemployment rate								
Registered[3]	4.3	5.3	5.6	5.7	5.7	5.3	4.7	4.7
Standardised rate (Eurostat definition)	..	3.9	4.4	4.4	4.5	4.0	3.7	3.7

1. Contribution to change in GDP (as a percentage of real GDP in the previous period).
2. Average of 1988-94 instead of 1984-94.
3. As a percentage of the total labour force including self-employment.
Source: OECD.

occurred on account of the strong increase in oil and other import prices and indirect tax hikes in mid-2000. Exports maintained most of their strong momentum in the first half of 2000 before decelerating in the second half and into 2001 in line with slower world trade growth (Table 1). Overall investment continued to grow in line with the economy with somewhat stronger growth in equipment and machinery investment having been offset by weaker construction investment as both housing and non-residential construction slowed. In 2001 the weakness of the economy was reinforced by the negative confidence effects following the 11 September terrorist attacks in the United States.

Growth slowed as exports decelerated

The strong expansion of exports in the first part of 2000 took place against the background of an improvement of external competitiveness and strongly accelerating export market growth, which for the year as a whole was almost twice as high in 2000 than the year before. However, in the second half of 2000 export growth decelerated, as the US economy slowed abruptly, which together with higher energy prices depressed the European business cycle with adverse effects on demand for Austrian produced goods. In the first half of 2001 export growth stood at half the rate of the year before. Foreign orders peaked in late 2000, before declining in the first half of 2001, roughly in line with the development of goods exports (Figure 3). Export growth was fairly evenly distributed across Austria's important trading partners, and with a noticeable acceleration of exports to the Eastern European countries following the previous years' slowdown in the wake of the Russian crisis. Similarly, in the first half of 2001 there was a slowdown in exports to most of the important markets (Table 2).

Competitiveness improved as the euro lost more than a fourth of its value against the US dollar between early 1999 and late 2000, although this trend did not continue in 2001. However, the real effective exchange rate depreciated less over the same period, reflecting the relatively low share of trade with the United States and rather similar inflation developments internationally. Productivity grew stronger than wages in 2000, contributing to falling relative unit labour costs in the manufacturing sector (Figure 4). The terms of trade deteriorated in 2000, as import prices increased at twice the rate of export prices, and continued to deteriorate in the first half of 2001. In combination with imports decelerating by less than exports, this led to a deterioration of the trade balance and the tourist balance also worsened (arising from high imports of tourist services). However, these developments were offset by an improvement in the transfer and income balances, so that, overall, the current account deficit came down to below 3 per cent of GDP (Table 3).

Private consumption stabilised growth in 2000

Private consumption increased by 2¾ per cent in 2000, but was losing pace during the year as increasing consumer price inflation restrained real income growth. Disposable nominal household income was underpinned by robust employment growth and higher wages as well as faster increases in non-wage income and income tax cuts. Consumer confidence began to weaken in early 2000 as consumer price inflation began to rise. It only recovered in early 2001 in the wake of the decline in oil prices and lower long-term interest rates, allowing for some stabilisation of private consumption growth at an annual rate of 1½ per cent in the first half of the year. Prospects of further increases in child benefits may also have played a role. However, since mid-2001 consumer confidence declined. Other consumption indicators, such as car purchases and retail sales, along with higher income taxation were also pointing to a deteriorating environment for pri-

Figure 3. **Business sector indicators**

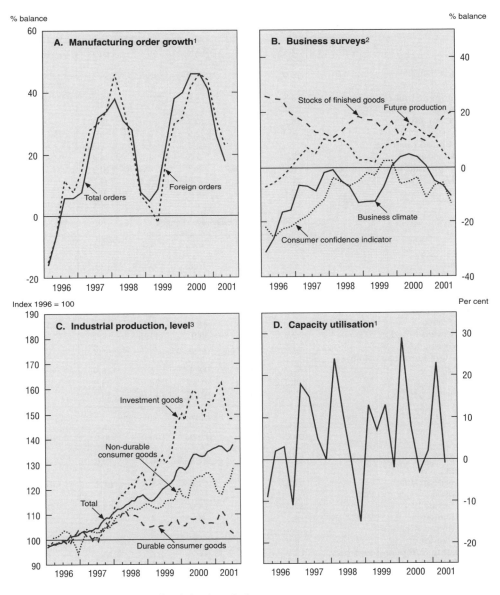

% balance

% balance

A. Manufacturing order growth[1]

Foreign orders

Total orders

B. Business surveys[2]

Stocks of finished goods

Future production

Business climate

Consumer confidence indicator

Index 1996 = 100

Per cent

C. Industrial production, level[3]

Investment goods

Non-durable consumer goods

Total

Durable consumer goods

D. Capacity utilisation[1]

1. Balance of positive-negative replies. *Industrievereinigung.*
2. Seasonally adjusted. Balance of positive-negative replies.
3. 3-month moving average.
Source: Austrian Institute for Economic Research (WIFO) and OECD, *Main Economic Indicators.*

Table 2.   **Austrian exports by destination**

	1996	1997	1998	1999	2000	2001 SI
	Billion euro[1]					
Total	44.5	51.9	56.4	60.1	69.4	72.0
of which:						
Europe	35.9	41.4	45.8	48.6	55.3	57.9
of which:						
European Union	28.5	32.2	36.0	37.8	42.5	45.1
of which:						
Germany	16.6	18.2	20.3	21.0	23.2	24.3
France	1.9	2.1	2.5	2.7	3.1	3.3
United Kingdom	1.6	2.2	2.4	2.6	3.0	3.2
Switzerland	2.2	2.5	2.8	3.6	4.4	4.5
Eastern European countries[2]	6.1	7.9	8.3	8.6	10.2	10.3
NAFTA	1.8	2.4	2.8	3.3	4.1	4.2
Japan	0.7	0.7	0.5	0.7	0.9	0.9
Far-east	1.5	1.6	1.4	1.7	2.1	2.1
	Percentage changes					Year-on-year
Total	5.4	16.7	8.6	6.6	15.5	6.2
of which:						
Europe	4.4	15.3	10.8	6.1	13.6	5.4
of which:						
European Union	2.7	13.0	11.8	4.8	12.4	6.7
of which:						
Germany	2.9	9.5	11.2	3.7	10.3	6.3
France	1.6	12.6	18.1	5.4	15.0	10.9
United Kingdom	12.9	36.7	9.9	11.6	14.9	5.1
Switzerland	−3.8	14.8	11.4	27.9	22.8	−4.4
Eastern European countries[2]	12.7	29.4	4.2	3.9	18.9	6.6
NAFTA	15.7	31.0	18.4	16.6	26.9	9.6
Japan	24.2	−5.0	−19.7	38.9	24.9	9.8
Far-east	2.7	6.3	−10.0	18.9	28.2	14.1
	Share per cent total					
Total	100.0	100.0	100.0	100.0	100.0	100.0
of which:						
Europe	80.7	79.7	81.3	80.9	79.6	80.4
of which:						
European Union	64.2	62.1	63.9	62.8	61.1	62.6
of which:						
Germany	37.4	35.1	35.9	35.0	33.4	33.7
France	4.3	4.1	4.5	4.4	4.4	4.6
United Kingdom	3.5	4.1	4.2	4.4	4.4	4.4
Switzerland	4.9	4.9	5.0	6.0	6.4	6.2
Eastern European countries[2]	13.8	15.3	14.7	14.3	14.7	14.3
NAFTA	4.1	4.6	5.0	5.4	6.0	5.8
Japan	1.5	1.3	0.9	1.2	1.3	1.2
Far-east	3.3	3.0	2.5	2.8	3.1	2.8

1.   €1 = Sch 13.7603.
2.   Bulgaria, Estonia, Latvia, Lithuania, Romania, Russia, Slovakia, Slovenia, Ukrania, Czech Republic, Hungary and Poland.
Source: OECD, *Foreign Trade Statistics, Series* A.

Figure 4. **Indicators of competitiveness**
Index 1991 =100

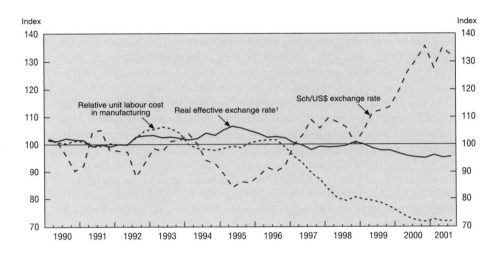

1. Deflated by the CPI.
Source: OECD.

Table 3. **Current account of the balance of payments**
Billion euro[1]

	1996	1997	1998	1999	2000	2001 S1[2]
Goods and services	−2.1	−2.9	−1.2	−1.7	−1.9	−1.6
Goods, net	−5.6	−3.8	−3.3	−3.4	−3.0	−2.8
Exports	44.6	52.0	56.4	60.5	70.2	73.2
Imports	50.2	55.8	59.7	63.9	73.2	76.0
Services, net	3.5	0.9	2.1	1.6	1.0	1.2
Exports	23.1	24.6	26.5	29.4	32.8	31.9
Imports	19.6	23.7	24.4	27.7	31.8	30.7
Investment income, net	−0.7	−1.3	−1.8	−2.7	−2.4	−3.2
Transfers, net	−1.4	−1.5	−1.7	−1.9	−1.3	−1.3
Government	−1.1	−1.4	−1.3	−1.4	−1.1	−1.0
Other transfers	−0.2	−0.1	−0.4	−0.5	−0.2	−0.2
Current account	−4.2	−5.8	−4.7	−6.3	−5.7	−6.0
Per cent of GDP	−2.3	−3.2	−2.5	−3.2	−2.8	−2.8

1. €1 = Sch 13.7603.
2. Seasonally adjusted and annualised.
Source: Oesterreichische Nationalbank (OeBN) and OECD.

vate consumption. In the past, households have adjusted their savings rate in times of transitory income variation to smooth out spending. While this would underpin private consumption in the remainder of 2001, the negative confidence effects emanating from the terrorist attacks are likely to counteract this effect.

Total investment, normally rather sensitive to the business cycle, grew at the same rate as the economy in 2000. This development reflects relatively stronger growth in machinery and equipment investment, particularly in the first half of the year. However, the growth of investment in machinery and equipment slowed in the second half of 2000 and the first half of 2001, reflecting deteriorating export prospects. An additional factor in 2001 is the abolition of an investment subsidy ("Investitionsfreibetrag"). Business surveys revealed a significant deterioration of the business climate with orders coming down and production expectations declining. Growing stocks and a falling capacity utilisation together with the negative confidence effects from the terrorist attacks point to continued weakness of the investment climate for machinery and equipment (Figure 3). Construction investment was weak throughout 2000 and in the first half of 2001 as business sentiment deteriorated and housing demand remained weak. Moreover, construction intention surveys point to a further reduction of activity in the remaining part of 2001, including a contraction of investment by utilities.[3] The high share of construction investment and an excess supply of housing – following high activity in the 1990s and depressed demand in line with demographic changes including a sharp decline in immigration – suggest a further downsizing of the sector (Figure 5).

Employment continued to grow, although at a slowing pace

Overall employment growth slowed from an annual rate of 1¾ per cent in the second semester of 1999 to ½ per cent in the second half of 2000, and while the overall growth rate was slightly higher in the first half of 2001 the pace of employment creation was losing its momentum during the semester (Figure 6, Panel A). Most of the employment growth took place in the private service sector, with a substantial part of overall employment creation taking place in the form of part-time employment. Indeed, in 2000 employment growth in full-time equivalents was only about two-thirds of the per head count.[4] Within the service sector, the business related services maintained their high pace of employment creation throughout 2000 and into 2001 – partly reflecting continued outsourcing of services from the industry sector and ongoing east-west integration – but employment growth decelerated sharply in the second quarter. Employment growth in other service sectors was considerably weaker already in 2000. This reflects relatively robust private consumption on the one hand and the negative public employment effects on account of the fiscal consolidation programme on the other hand. The contraction of employment in the construction sector continued during 2000

Figure 5. **Investment in selected OECD countries**[1]
Per cent of GDP

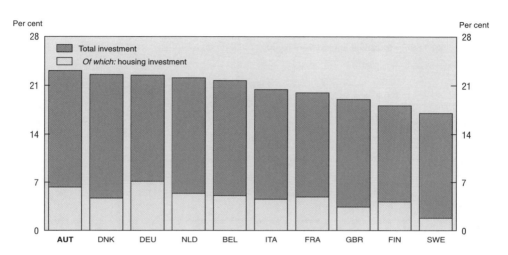

1. In 2000.
Source: OECD, *National Accounts.*

and in the first half of 2001, in line with the low rate of activity in the sector. Employment in the manufacturing sector (seasonally adjusted) began to increase in early 2000 and continued increasing at an accelerating rate during the year. However, with the demand outlook deteriorating, particularly on foreign markets, the pace of the sector's employment creation fell in the first half of 2001. Productivity growth doubled in 2000 and remained strong in the first half of 2001.

The labour force is still increasing, albeit slowly, as the negative demographic effects of ageing are more than offset by higher labour force participation (particularly for females and immigrant workers). The increase in the – relatively low – female labour force participation rate is mainly related to the increase in part-time job openings being occupied by females entering the labour force. With employment growing faster than the labour force the unemployment rate declined by ½ percentage point (seasonally adjusted) to 4½ per cent (national accounts) between late 1999 and late 2000 – a level last attained a decade ago. However, the slowing of employment creation in 2001 caused a slight increase in the unemployment rate thereafter. Other indicators coming in after mid-2001 point to a continuing weakening of the labour market with the number of unfilled vacancies falling and a further increase in the seasonally-adjusted registered unemployment rate (Figure 6, Panel B).

Figure 6.   **Employment, unemployment and the labour force**
Seasonally adjusted

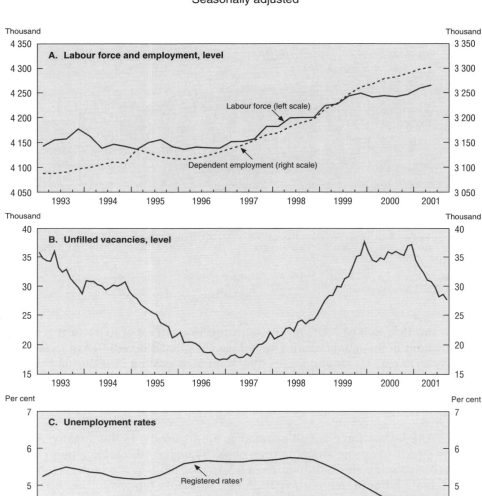

1. Registered unemployment as a per cent of total labour force including self-employment.
2. Eurostat definition.
Source: Austrian Institute for Economic Research (WIFO) and OECD, *Main Economic Indicators*.

Unemployment has declined for most groups on the labour market in 2000, although the general deterioration of the labour market during the first half of 2001 led to some reversals. The female unemployment rate has come down to more or less the same level as male unemployment, reflecting a larger decline in the female rate as a result of the stronger employment demand in the service sectors than in the traditionally more male dominated manufacturing and construction sectors. Long-term unemployment (defined as more than 12 months of unemployment) almost halved between 1999 and 2000 and continued to fall in the first three quarters of 2001, accounting for only 6 per cent of registered unemployment in September 2001, down from 10½ per cent the year before. This can partly be accounted for by an increased utilisation of active labour market programs (ALMPs), which are largely targeted at the long-term unemployed (see Chapter III). The upswing also benefited difficult-to-employ groups (mainly handicapped people) with a tangible lowering of their unemployment into spring 2001. Unemployment for the age group above 50 years also declined, but has started to climb again. The youth unemployment rate – already low by international standards – fell to 5¼ per cent in early 2001, partly for demographic reasons. It increased, however, by ½ percentage point the following half year. On the other hand, unemployment among foreigners has remained high over the past couple of years.

Despite the tightening of the labour market in 2000, wage developments remained subdued with collectively bargained wages increasing by 2.1 per cent and only slightly faster increases in the average compensation per employee, indicating that until now second-round effects of the acceleration in consumer price inflation on wages have largely been avoided (Table 4). The background for

Table 4.   **Wages and prices**

Annual growth, per cent

	1984-94 average	1995	1996	1997	1998	1999	2000
Productivity per employee, total economy	1.7	1.6	2.6	1.1	2.7	1.4	2.1
Compensation per employee	4.7	3.5	1.1	0.6	2.8	2.0	2.2
Unit labour costs, total economy	3.3	2.5	−1.0	−0.1	0.4	0.9	0.5
Compensation per employee, business sector	4.8	3.5	0.8	2.3	2.7	1.5	2.3
Unit labour costs, business sector	2.8	1.1	−2.0	0.6	−0.2	−0.1	−0.5
Wages in industry,[1] hourly rates	5.1	3.7	3.3	2.4	2.6	2.9	2.4
Unit labour costs, manufacturing	2.2	−0.6	−0.8	−4.4	−1.7	−0.5	−6.0
GDP deflator	3.1	2.5	1.3	0.9	0.5	0.7	1.2
Private consumption deflator	2.9	2.0	1.9	1.5	0.5	0.7	1.5

1.   Industry, including construction and electricity.
Source: OECD and Austrian Institute for Economic Research (WIFO).

moderate wage negotiation settlements in autumn 1999 was an expected continuation of the then observed low consumer price inflation. With the latter accelerating subsequently, realised real wage growth was zero or slightly negative in 2000.
As unions accepted a trade-off between low wage growth in exchange for better
employment prospects, the wage settlements for 2001 only led to somewhat
higher increases in collectively bargained wages (about ½ percentage point). In
the process, increases in negotiated wages levelled off at around 2¾ per cent after
mid-2001 and first indications from this autumn's wage negotiation round point to
only slightly higher increases for 2002.

Inflation has increased, primarily on the back of higher import prices, but is coming down

Consumer price inflation picked up at the beginning of 1999, as the effects
of the stronger US dollar combined with higher oil prices led to increasing energy
costs and import prices, but remained in the lower range of EU inflation rates
(Figure 7). Until mid-2000 the acceleration was more or less equal to that in other
European countries, but higher indirect taxes – implemented as part of the fiscal
consolidation programme – then lifted the rate of consumer price increases by
another ½ percentage point to about 2¾ per cent. In 2001, consumer price inflation peaked at 3¼ per cent in May, before falling to 2.6 per cent in September. The
decline was driven by lower oil and import prices and the effects of the previous
year's higher indirect taxes falling out of the index. Core inflation (excluding
energy and food items from the consumer price index), however, increased
because of higher rates for rents and services inflation (Figure 7, Panel B). An
additional factor behind the increase in consumer price inflation in the first
months of 2001 were higher food prices, which were mostly related to the mad cow
and foot and mouth scares in 2000 and related substitution effects.[5] These effects
began to fade in late spring 2001.

Monetary conditions have not acted to restrain growth. In 2000, the depreciation of the exchange rate contributed to an easing of monetary conditions,
while on the other hand increases in policy rates by the European Central Bank
triggered significant increases in short-term market rates (Figure 8). Long-term
interest rates have been stable until the end of 2000, when they came down in line
with US rates, primarily in reaction to a slowdown of economic activity internationally. During the first half of 2001, monetary conditions were roughly unchanged.
Short-term rates declined with the ECB's 25 basis point cut in policy rates in
spring 2001, while long-term interest rates remained fairly stable. Reflecting the
increase in inflation both real long- and short-term rates – measured as nominal
rates minus current inflation – stand at around the lowest levels over the past
decade. Moreover, the exchange rate vis-à-vis the US dollar remained roughly

Figure 7. **Consumer price inflation**

Percentage changes from previous year

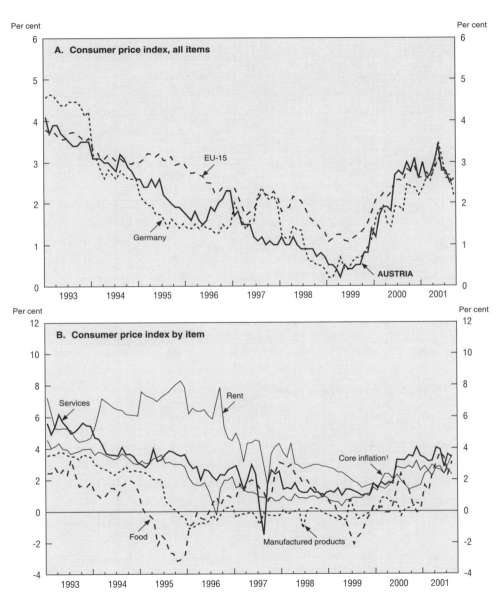

1. CPI net food and energy (OECD definition).
Source: Austrian Institute for Economic Research (WIFO) and OECD, *Main Economic Indicators*.

Figure 8. **Interest rate developments**

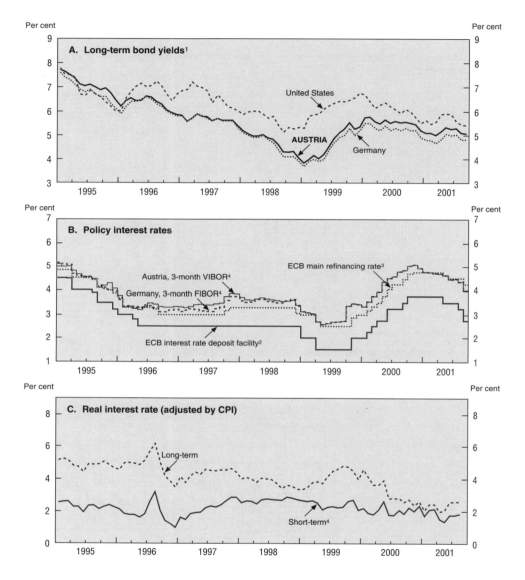

1. Austria: 10-year benchmark bond; Germany: yields on listed federal securities with residual maturities of 9 to 10 years; United States: US government bonds (composite over 10 years).
2. Before January 1999, discount rate.
3. Before January 1999, German repo rate.
4. From January 1999, VIBOR and FIBOR have been replaced by EURIBOR.
Source: Oesterreichische Nationalbank (OeNB); Deutsche Bundesbank and OECD, *Main Economic Indicators*.

unchanged, as it has fluctuated around its average level of 2000. Following the 11 September terrorist attacks in the United States, monetary conditions became accommodative as the ECB reduced policy rates in steps by 1 percentage point.

Short-term prospects and risks

Growth in 2001 is likely to be markedly lower than the year before, dropping to a rate significantly below potential in the OECD's projections. This reflects the deceleration in world trade and slowing domestic demand that have been evident during the course of the year, and this weakness is now reinforced by the negative global growth shock emanating from the terrorist attacks on the United States. Adverse confidence effects of this event are projected to weaken global activity and trade well into the first half next year. But world trade growth may begin to strengthen again thereafter, leading to a progressive pick-up in Austrian activity which will also be supported by more vigorous domestic demand. Monetary conditions are projected to support growth.

Table 5.   **Economic projections to 2003**

Percentage change from previous period

	2000	2001[1]	2002[1]	2003[1]
Private consumption	2.5	1.5	1.8	2.4
Government consumption	0.9	−0.6	0.6	0.5
Gross fixed investment	5.1	−0.5	0.3	3.6
Construction	0.3	−2.9	−1.0	2.6
Machinery and equipment	11.1	2.1	1.7	4.6
Changes in stocks[2]	−0.3	0.1	0.0	0.0
Total domestic demand	2.5	0.7	1.2	2.3
Foreign balance[2]	0.5	0.4	0.3	0.4
Exports of goods and services	12.2	5.3	3.8	7.0
Imports of goods and services	11.1	4.6	3.3	6.3
Gross domestic product	3.0	1.2	1.5	2.7
Memorandum items:				
Private consumption deflator	1.5	2.6	1.8	1.9
GDP deflator	1.2	2.0	1.8	1.9
Total employment[3]	0.9	0.4	−0.2	0.3
Unemployment (registered)	4.7	4.8	5.3	5.1
Household saving ratio	7.8	7.3	6.6	6.5
Export market growth[4]	13.7	2.4	3.2	7.9
Short-term interest rate	4.4	4.2	3.0	3.8
Long-term interest rate	5.6	5.1	4.9	5.3
General government budget balance, per cent of GDP	−1.1	0.0	−0.4	0.1
Current balance, per cent of GDP	−2.8	−2.5	−1.9	−1.5

1. Projections.
2. Contributions to changes in GDP (as a percentage of real GDP in the previous period).
3. Including self-employment.
4. Manufactured goods.
Source: OECD.

Indeed, private consumption is likely to recover as consumer confidence stabilises, driven by rising disposable incomes, rises in family benefits and improving terms of trade. Investment in machinery and equipment should also gather momentum, following the improvement in external demand. Construction will remain subdued in 2002 but should strengthen thereafter. Government consumption is projected to slow, owing to ongoing fiscal consolidation that should reduce growth by ¼ percentage point in 2002. All in all, GDP growth is projected to rebound in the second half of next year and to accelerate further in 2003, allowing the output gap, that is opening in 2001 and 2002, to begin to close again (Table 5).

Large uncertainties surround this projection. On the downside, there is a risk not only from the external side but also because a further deterioration of domestic confidence could markedly restrain private consumption growth or further postpone investment projects. On the upside, Austria would of course benefit from a faster-than-projected recovery in Germany, its largest trading partner, although business and consumer sentiment has deteriorated there leaving considerable uncertainties as to the timing of any pick-up.

II. Fiscal policy: consolidation to be associated with reform

Fiscal consolidation in Austria came to a halt in 1998 and 1999 as short-term consolidation measures contained in an earlier savings package had not been replaced sufficiently by longer term structural policies, and new spending demands were arising. In 2000 implementation of the federal budget was delayed due to the transition phase associated with establishing the new government after the general elections. In combination with tax cuts and phased increases in family benefits that became effective in January 2000, this adversely affected the general government budget. Nevertheless, the general government deficit dropped by about 1 per cent of GDP, to 1.1 per cent, owing to higher annual growth, under-spending on a number of budget items, one-off receipts from the auctioning of UMTS mobile phone licenses and sales of real estate, and revenue-raising measures installed by the new administration to contain the deficit. The government has committed itself to balancing the general government budget but has also adopted policy initiatives that require increased spending. A number of structural measures have already been implemented designed to achieve the consolidation goal and improve the functioning of the public sector, and others have been announced. Mainly, envisaged policies comprise pension reform, public sector reform, better targeting of social benefits and increases in taxation, to some extent via broadening the tax base. Most of these initiatives go in the right direction and would accelerate the pace of structural reform if they were fully implemented. However, a substantial part of fiscal consolidation is being generated by one-off measures on the revenue side, which will have to be replaced by longer-term structural policies to improve general government finances in a durable way as planned. Moreover, it will be necessary to go further with respect to reforming social entitlement spending, public sector reform and pension reform.

The first part of this chapter reviews recent budgetary developments and considers the prospect for continued fiscal consolidation in view of the envisaged savings package and slower economic growth than in recent years. The second part highlights major structural policy issues that will shape the stance of fiscal policy in the medium term, namely pension reform, administrative reform and inter-state revenue sharing.

The 1999 budget: fiscal consolidation at a halt

No progress in fiscal consolidation was made in 1999. The general government deficit came in at 2.1 per cent of GDP (national accounts definition), just 0.1 percentage point lower than in the year before and the structural deficit remained unchanged (Table 6). General government debt increased in terms of GDP to 64.9 per cent, after 63.9 per cent in the year before (Maastricht definition). The debt level was boosted by the portfolio re-evaluation of part of Austria's foreign currency debt, which followed the appreciation of the Japanese yen and the Swiss franc.

Outlays for wages rose due to both higher wage settlements and structural changes in employment patterns, with the former reflecting some catch-up from

Table 6.   **Net lending of the general government**
National accounts basis, billion of euro[1]

	1996	1997	1998	1999	2000	2001[2]	2002[2]	2003[2]
Current receipts	85.7	87.4	90.7	93.0	95.9	101.1	102.8	106.7
Total direct taxes	23.3	24.6	25.9	26.3	27.4	30.9	31.4	32.8
Households	19.4	20.6	21.6	22.4	22.7	24.8	25.8	26.8
Business	4.0	4.0	4.3	3.9	4.7	6.1	5.6	6.0
Total indirect taxes	25.8	27.1	28.3	29.5	30.1	31.5	32.0	33.4
Social security	31.1	31.7	32.8	34.0	35.1	36.0	36.9	38.1
Other current transfer received	2.4	2.6	2.8	2.8	2.7	2.3	2.2	2.1
Property and entrepreneurial income	3.1	1.4	0.9	0.3	0.5	0.4	0.4	0.4
Current disbursements	87.7	86.8	90.1	92.7	95.2	97.7	98.9	101.3
Government consumption	36.1	35.9	37.2	38.7	39.7	40.3	40.9	41.9
of which: Wages and salaries	22.0	21.0	21.6	22.6	23.3	23.6	23.8	24.3
Interest on public debt	7.5	7.1	7.2	6.9	7.2	6.8	6.9	7.0
Subsidies	4.7	4.7	5.3	5.1	5.3	5.9	6.0	6.2
Social security paid	34.6	34.6	35.3	36.9	38.5	39.0	40.3	41.3
Other transfers paid	4.7	4.6	5.2	5.1	4.5	5.1	4.9	5.0
Net capital outlays	4.8	4.0	5.1	4.6	3.0	4.0	4.7	5.1
Gross investment	5.1	3.6	3.5	3.6	3.5	3.4	3.4	3.5
Net capital transfers	−3.6	−3.4	−4.6	−4.1	−2.6	−3.8	−4.6	−4.9
Consumption of fixed capital	3.8	3.0	3.0	3.1	3.1	3.2	3.3	3.3
Net lending	−6.8	−3.4	−4.5	−4.3	−2.3	−0.1	−0.8	0.3
Per cent of GDP	−3.8	−1.9	−2.4	−2.2	−1.1	0.0	−0.4	0.1
Gross debt (Maastricht basis)	123.0	118.1	121.4	127.5	130.0	129.9	130.8	131.0
Per cent of GDP	69.1	64.7	63.9	64.9	63.5	61.5	59.9	57.4
Structural budget balance	−6.5	−2.9	−4.5	−4.5	−3.8	0.0	−0.2	0.7
Per cent of potential GDP	−3.6	−1.6	−2.4	−2.3	−1.9	0.0	−0.1	0.3

1. €1 = Sch 13.7603.
2. Projections.
Source: OECD.

earlier years when subdued public-sector wages contributed to fiscal restraint. Major extensions of social benefit programmes also added to higher expenditure. In response to a ruling of the Constitutional Court, which found the existing system of family taxation unconstitutional, child benefits were increased in terms of both extended tax credits and cash benefits paid from the Family Burden Equalisation Fund (Familienlastenausgleichsfonds, FLAF).[6] The National Action Plan for Employment required additional budgetary resources of the federal government, in particular for extended active labour market programmes. Moreover, federal transfers to the pension system grew larger than budgeted. Due to these pressures, overall federal expenditure accelerated, although interest payments on government debt turned out significantly lower than budgeted (Table 7). Shortfalls in some revenue items contributed to the pressure on the general government balance. While wage tax receipts came in higher than expected, the opposite was true for the value-added tax. Moreover, business tax receipts dropped by 10 per cent compared with the 1998 outturn (budgetary definition), partly on account of business losses from earlier years carried over into 1999. This effect originates from the 1996/97 fiscal consolidation package which suspended for 1997 and 1998 the possibility of deducting from profits losses that were incurred in the past and carried forwards. The act included the option to shift forward the losses to 1999. On the other hand, higher than budgeted one-off receipts, such as revenues from selling a mobile phone license, helped containing the deficit.

The 2000 budget outcome: containing the deficit

In January 2000 tax relief measures and the second phase of the family benefits package came into force, both having been legislated in 1999. The tax measures aimed at lowering income taxes, in particular for low-income households, raising child benefits and fostering the attractiveness of Austria as a business location (see Box 1 and the 1999 Survey). Implementation of the federal budget was delayed on account of the transition phase associated with forming a new government after the general elections in October 1999. The new government, which came into power in February 2000, was confronted with time pressure to present a budget and have it passed by parliament. The tax relief measures and the family package threatened to significantly increase the general budget deficit. A provisional budget arrangement, based on the estimates of 1999, came automatically into force in January 2000 until the end of May, restraining the consolidation process. In June, the new budget law for 2000 came into effect. In conjunction with the 2000 budget law a package of revenue raising measures was implemented designed to contain the deficit and provide a base for further consolidation steps. Mainly, the package consists of increases in indirect taxes – the tobacco tax, vehicle insurance tax, levy on electricity – and fees, but sales of real estate also contributed to generating revenues (Box 1). Discretionary spending

Table 7.   **The Federal budget**[1]

Cash basis, adjusted; billion of euro[2]

	1997	1998	1999		2000		2001	2002
	Outturn	Outturn	Budget	Outturn	Budget	Outturn	Budget	Budget
Revenue[1]	45.8	47.3	47.4	47.4	48.5	49.9	52.7	54.0
(Percentage change)	(4.3)	(3.2)	(0.0)	(0.0)	(2.3)	(5.3)	(5.6)	(3.7)
Taxes before revenue sharing	45.3	48.7	49.5	48.7	49.8	50.4	54.5	56.8
Wage tax	13.3	14.1	14.4	14.8	14.1	14.5	16.1	17.1
Taxes on other income and profit	6.3	6.9	6.5	6.2	6.5	6.7	7.7	8.1
Value-added tax	15.1	15.7	17.0	16.5	17.1	17.1	17.9	18.5
Major excise taxes[3]	3.5	3.7	3.7	3.9	3.9	3.9	4.0	3.3
Other taxes	7.2	8.4	8.0	7.4	8.1	8.2	8.8	9.1
Minus tax-sharing transfers	13.0	13.4	14.0	13.9	14.1	15.3	15.7	16.4
Minus transfers to EU budget	2.3	1.9	2.3	2.1	2.4	2.1	2.4	2.4
Taxes after revenue sharing	30.0	33.4	33.2	32.7	33.3	33.0	36.5	38.0
Taxes transfers to federal funds	1.4	1.4	1.5	1.4	1.5	1.5	1.5	1.6
Tax-like revenue[4]	6.2	6.5	6.6	6.8	6.8	6.9	7.1	7.4
Federal enterprises	0.1	0.1	0.0	0.0	–	–	–	–
Other revenue	8.1	5.9	6.1	6.4	6.8	8.4	7.6	7.1
Expenditure[1]	50.5	51.3	52.8	52.2	53.0	52.4	55.4	55.2
(Percentage change)	(–0.2)	(1.5)	(3.0)	(1.9)	(1.5)	(0.3)	(5.7)[13]	(–0.3)[14]
Wages and salaries[5]	10.0	10.2	10.3	10.7	10.8	10.7	11.0	10.8
Pensions[6]	2.8	2.9	3.1	3.0	3.1	3.1	3.2	3.3
Current expenditure on goods[7]	4.5	4.7	4.8	4.7	4.6	4.7	5.2	5.3
Gross investment	0.7	0.8	0.8	0.7	0.6	0.5	0.8	0.5
Transfer payments	24.4	25.3	25.7	25.8	25.8	25.2	26.8	27.0
Family allowances	3.9	3.7	3.9	3.8	4.0	4.0	4.1	4.4
Unemployment benefits	2.4	2.5	2.4	2.4	2.3	2.3	2.0	2.0
Transfers to the social security system[8]	7.1	7.5	7.5	7.8	7.6	7.3	7.8	8.0
Transfers to enterprises[9]	4.0	4.0	4.4	4.0	4.2	4.1	5.2	4.9
Other transfers[10]	7.0	7.6	7.5	7.7	7.7	7.5	7.8	7.8
Interest[11]	6.4	6.3	7.2	6.6	7.2	7.0	7.5	7.4
Other expenditure[12]	1.6	1.1	0.9	0.8	1.0	1.2	0.8	0.8
Net balance	–4.7	–4.0	–5.4	–4.9	–4.5	–2.5	–2.7	–1.2
(in per cent of GDP)	(–2.6)	(–2.1)	(–2.7)	(–2.5)	(–2.2)	(–1.2)	(–1.3)	(–0.5)
Memorandum item:								
Net balance, administrative basis	–4.9	–4.8	–5.1	–5.0	–4.0	–2.9	–2.4	–0.8
(in per cent of GDP)	(–2.7)	(–2.5)	(–2.6)	(–2.5)	(–2.0)	(–1.4)	(–1.1)	(–0.4)

1. Adjusted for double counting.
2. €1 = Sch 13.7603.
3. Mineral oil and tobacco taxes.
4. Mainly contributions to unemployment insurance and to the fund for family allowances.
5. Including contribution to salaries of teachers employed by the states.
6. Pensions of federal civil servants and contribution to pensions of teachers employed by the states.
7. Including investment expenditure on defense.
8. Mainly to the general pension system (ASVG).
9. Including agriculture.
10. Including transfers to other levels of government, from 1995 onwards also including transfers to EU.
11. Including commissions and management fees and provisions for interest on zero coupon bonds, also including interest on swap transactions.
12. Including reserve operations except federal funds.
13. Change over 2000 outturn.
14. Change over 2001 budget.
Source: Ministry of Finance.

Box 1. Recent tax measures

Tax reform measures that came into force in 2000 originate from two different tax reforms. The reform of the previous government, legislated in 1998 and 1999, aimed at lowering income taxes, in particular for low-income households, raising child benefits and fostering the attractiveness of Austria as a business location. Most tax measures associated with this reform came into force in January 2000, while phased increases in child benefits became effective in 1999 and 2000. The subsequent tax package was part of the 2000 budget plan of the new government and aimed at reducing the government deficit by raising indirect taxes. Most of these measures came into force in June 2000.

A. The 1999 income and business tax reform

1. *Personal income tax reductions*

Subsistence income of up to Sch 50 000 (€ 3 634) per year was made tax-free, and statutory tax rates in the personal income tax code were lowered by 1 percentage point for annual incomes of up to Sch 700 000 (€ 50 871). The lowest tax rate is now 21 per cent, increasing in steps to 41 per cent for up to Sch 700 000 (€ 50 871) per year, and totalling 50 per cent for incomes of Sch 700 000 (€ 50 871) and higher. The standard tax credit has been increased and made digressive. The tax relief of these measures amounts to Sch 17 billion (€ 1.246 billion) (government estimate, 2000).

Furthermore, tax concessions were introduced for contributions to voluntary pension schemes and voluntary payments made by employers to dismissed workers covered by a social plan.

2. *Family allowances*

Benefits for children have been increased in two steps, 1999 and 2000, totalling Sch 12 billion (€ 0.876 billion) (compared with 1998).

3. *Business taxation*

Several tax measures were implemented aiming at increasing the attractiveness of Austria as a business location and at promoting employment. Major measures are:

- Notional interest on additional equity is taken into consideration in the determination of taxable profits and taxed at a final rate of 25 per cent.
- Higher tax allowance for research and development.
- Tax allowance for training apprentices (until 2003).
- Tax allowance for training of employees.
- Tax concessions for young entrepreneurs starting an enterprise (until 2003).

Box I.   **Recent tax measures** (*cont.*)

– Introduction of a tax break of Sch 5 million (€ 0.36 million) for inheritance and gift taxes for enterprises being passed on to successors.
– Abolition of the mineral oil tax for the utilisation of environment-friendly fuel based on rape seed alcohol.
–   The business tax measures amount to a tax relief of Sch 3.5 billion (€ 0.25 billion) (2000). Overall, the tax reform package (including the family benefits) aimed at reducing the tax burden by Sch 32.5 billion (€ 2.36 billion) in 2000 (1.2 per cent of GDP).

B.   The tax package of June 2000

The following indirect taxes have been increased:
– Tobacco tax.
– Levy on electricity.
– Increase of the vehicle insurance tax.
– Certain fees (*e.g.* for passports and other official documents).

These measures imply additional revenues of some Sch 7 billion (€ 0.51 billion) in 2000, and Sch 11 billion (€ 0.80 billion) in 2001.

C.   The "Capital market campaign"

In autumn 2000, the government adopted several measures to promote the Austrian capital market. The most important tax measures were:
– The stock exchange turnover tax was abolished as of 1 October 2000.
– The threshold for the annual tax-free issuance of shares to own employees was raised from Sch 10 000 (€ 727) to Sch 20 000 (€ 1 453).
– Value increases of stock options up to a maximum of Sch 500 000 (€ 36 336) were partly tax-exempted.
– To compensate for the revenue losses, the limit for tax-free sales of company holdings was reduced from minimum shares of 10 per cent down to 1 per cent of the company capital.

Further tax measures

– Due to a ruling of the EU court, taxation for beverages had to be reformed. The beverage tax was abolished, the revenue loss has partly been compensated by higher tax rates on alcoholics and the abolition of the VAT rate reduction on coffee and tea.
– The tax for advertising was decreased from 10 to 5 per cent and receipts re-allocated across the different levels of government.

was tightened. Moreover, measures were legislated to contain cost increases in the public pension system, and some of these measures, curbing the inflow into early retirement, became already effective in winter 2000 (see the section on pensions further below).

Federal expenditures in 2000 (cash basis) remained almost unchanged, significantly below the budget plan. Public sector wage growth was subdued, and investment was cut back, helped by the separation of business-like units from the budget. On the other hand, capital transfers to the Austrian Railways have increased substantially for the purpose of increasing investment in rail infrastructure. Similarly, substantial capital transfers were made to the Federal Estate Holding (*Bundes-Immobiliengesellschaft*, BIG), to enable the Holding to buy real estate from the federal government.Unemployment benefit payments also declined owing to further reductions in unemployment. Budgetary transfers to the public old-age pension system dropped well below the budget plan, but this is related to utilising reserves built up in other funds. Interest payments for federal government debt slid upwards, however, and this is largely attributable to higher debt servicing obligations for part of Austria's foreign currency debt implied by the revaluation of foreign currency. Wage tax revenues dropped compared with the year before on account of the income tax reductions, although receipts came in much higher than budgeted. Similarly, the business tax reductions implied that receipts in profit taxes were low, falling short of the receipts in 1998 (the 1999 outcome having been exceptionally low due to the special conditions for loss carry-overs) (Table 7). But substantial additional revenues were generated both by the auctioning of UMTS mobile phone licences and sales of real estate, which generated revenues of 0.4 and almost 0.2 per cent of GDP, respectively.

Overall, the general government deficit dropped by 1 percentage point to 1.1 per cent of GDP (national accounts definition), with the surplus of the states and communities remaining unchanged at 0.3 per cent and the deficit of the social security system increasing to 0.1 per cent of GDP, respectively (Table 8). While the

Table 8. **Budget deficit by government level**

National accounts basis, million euro[1]

	1997	1998	1999	2000
Federal government	−4 927	−5 516	−4 687	−2 907
States (excluding Vienna)	1046	828	523	509
Communities (including Vienna)	480	269	116	145
Social Security funds	305	174	−44	−109
General government	−3 096	−4 237	−4 091	−2 362
(As a percentage of GDP)	−1.7	−2.2	−2.1	−1.1

1. €1 = Sch 13.7603.
Source: Ministry of Finance.

budget outcome undershoots the deficit target of the stability programme (1.7 per cent of GDP) by more than ½ percentage point, more than half of the reduction in the deficit between 1999 and 2000 is attributable to the one-off receipts stemming from the sale of the UMTS licenses and real estate. The general government debt decreased by 1½ percentage points of GDP to 63.5 per cent (Maastricht definition).

The 2001 and 2002 budgets: towards a balanced budget

The federal budgets for 2001 and 2002 have been jointly presented, and were legislated in December 2000 and April 2001 respectively. Fiscal policies for this year and next aim at bridging two aspects that are not easily reconciled: implementing policy initiatives that are associated with higher spending, and establishing the general government deficit on a downwards path leading to a balanced budget. A number of programmes have been budgeted that will lead to higher spending. These comprise higher outlays for research and development and certain infrastructure projects, notably for universities and schools, and higher spending in favour of a better integration of disabled persons in the labour market. Higher subsidies to enterprises, partly relating to previous spin-offs of corporations from the government sector, have also been scheduled. Moreover, the government has decided to implement a further family support scheme (Kinderbetreuungsgeld), which will come into effect in 2002. The scheme replaces the previous insurance scheme (Karenzgeld) that gave child benefits to parents for a maximum period of two years after the birth of the child, provided the parent had worked prior to the child's birth. In the new scheme, benefits are given for three years, independently of whether or not the parent was working prior to the birth of the child. The level of the benefits was increased and the cap for supplementary earnings raised. Costs associated with the reform are estimated to total some € 908 million in the first year (0.44 per cent of GDP in 2000), increasing to € 1.25 billion by 2005. Simultaneously the government has embarked on a policy to renew fiscal consolidation. For this purpose a fiscal consolidation programme was presented that affects all levels of government. The goal is lowering the general government deficit to 0.75 per cent of GDP in 2001 and eliminating it next year. An arrangement has been made between the federal government, the states and the local governments obliging the Länder and the communities to produce a surplus of ¾ per cent of GDP and balance the budget, respectively, in 2001 and thereafter. A zero deficit is also envisaged for the social security system. The consolidation profile is based on the assumption that real GDP grows at a rate of 2.8 per cent in 2001 and 2.7 per cent in 2002. In the government's projections (April 2001), the deficit is mainly reduced from the revenue side, with general government receipts growing by 4.3 per cent in 2001 (net of the proceeds from selling the UMTS licenses in 2000) and 3.0 per cent in 2002.[7] General government spending is projected to grow at a rate of 2.3 per cent in 2001, somewhat higher than in 2000, before decelerating to a rate of 1.5 per cent in 2002.

The consolidation package, on which the federal budget laws for 2001 and 2002 have been based, contains both tax increases and measures of spending restraint (Table 9). On the expenditure side savings are to be generated from public sector reform (including reductions in government employment and already negotiated wage moderation), pension reform and tighter targeting of social benefits (see the discussion further below). These measures are envisaged to relieve the budget by some ½ per cent of GDP in 2001, and 1 per cent of GDP in 2002. While the pension reform measures and the tightening of certain social benefits have already been legislated, policies to improve the efficiency of the public sector have not all been decided yet. Several business-like units are planned to be separated from government budgets and put into the enterprise sector. This is true, for example, for hospitals of the states. The *Länder* also plan selling loans extended for the purpose of residential construction. For some of these operations, envisaged by the states, there is a risk that they might not conform with

Table 9. **Consolidation programme 2001-02**

Million euro [1]

	2001	2002
Expenditure side		
Public sector reform, including employment cuts and wage moderation	363	807
Pension reform, including civil servants	327	792
Benefit targeting, excluding higher family benefits	269	269
Transfers from off-budget funds	1 017	843
Austrian railway	153	218
Lower interest payments through debt reductions	0	218
Fiscal burden sharing with states and communities, including the full surplus of the states	2 035	2 035
Education and expenses for handicapped persons	−109	−145
Expenditures total	**4 055**	**5 036**
Revenue side		
Charges and measures broadening the tax base	2 260	2 391
Abolition of stock exchange turnover tax	−73	−73
Tax restaurant trade with 10 per cent VAT	−94	−116
Tuition fees for students	73	146
Higher dividend from the central bank	291	−
Revenues total	**2 456**	**2 275**
In per cent of consolidation	37.7	31.1
Consolidation total	**6 511**	**7 311**
In per cent of consolidation	100.0	100.0

1. €1 = Sch 13.7603.
Source: Ministry of Finance.

the principles laid down in the European System of National Accounting, and judgement by the statistical office of the EU, Eurostat, is pending. Tax measures comprise some tax increases – such as higher income taxation of foundations – and several measures designed to broaden the tax base, such as raising the depreciation period for buildings. There are also increases in charges. Some of the measures reduce tax exemptions or are elements of a broader reform programme. This holds for the introduction of tuition fees for students, which is part of the programme for reforming Austria's university system (see Chapter III below). Also, the stock exchange turnover tax has been abolished, which is welcome in that it supports strengthening equity financing in Austria. But overall, a more systematic approach to tax reform needs to be chosen. A significant part of the revenue raising measures in 2001 are one-off. The planned sales of loans by the states also belong to this category, as do further sales of real estate envisaged by the federal government. Increases in advance tax payments in 2001 are scheduled to be transformed into lasting revenue gains from 2002 on. In the federal budget, further relief is being generated by transferring surpluses from the Family Burden Equalisation Fund and the unemployment insurance fund to the public pension system. However, these reserve transactions – which are lacking transparency – do not contribute to reducing the general government deficit in terms of national accounting (Table 9).

It appears that budgetary positions have been assessed cautiously with relatively wide safety margins. Higher than expected business tax instalments and lower interest payments in late 2001 imply that a balanced budget is likely to be reached already in 2001. The discretionary measures of the savings programme have largely been implemented as far as 2001 is concerned. For 2002, the elements of the consolidation programme that have not yet been decided have a higher weight. Also, the projections are based on the assumption that the reductions in government employment do not increase the inflow into early retirement. Otherwise outlays would increase and tax increases are likely to follow. A risk to the projections arises from the conjunctural side. The sharp deceleration in economic activity has made it considerably more difficult to maintain balance in 2002. On current policies the general government balance is projected to exhibit a deficit of almost ½ per cent of GDP. Debt is projected to fall in 2001 and 2002, helped by privatisations.

Medium-term fiscal plans

The federal government has reinforced its commitment in the EU stability programme to continue fiscal consolidation and reduce the general government deficit in equal steps to zero by 2002, down from 1.1 per cent of GDP in 2000. In the years thereafter the general government budget is targeted to remain in balance while both revenues and spending in terms of GDP are scheduled to decline.

Table 10. **Medium-term fiscal objectives for the general government**
National accounts basis, per cent of GDP

	1999	2000	2001	2002	2003	2004
Budget deficit	−2.1	−1.4	−0.75	0.0	0.0	0.0
Primary balance	1.4	2.1	2.7	3.4	3.3	3.2
Revenues	51.5	50.4	50.2	50.0	49.6	49.4
Expenditures	53.7	51.8	50.9	50.0	49.6	49.4
Gross debt	64.6	63.1	61.4	59.1	57.2	55.3

Source: Austrian Government, Stability Programme of December 2000.

Gross debt (in the definition of the Maastricht Treaty) is to be reduced from some 63 per cent of GDP in 2000 to below 55½ per cent in 2004 (Table 10).

Continued fiscal consolidation is necessary – not least in view of the fact that the rapid demographic ageing in Austria will imply a heavy burden for general government finances over the next years to come – and the degree of consolidation is lagging behind what has been observed in many other OECD countries. Fiscal consolidation has the potential of improving growth prospects, and simulation studies for Austria indicate that balancing the general government budget would be associated with higher economic growth, compensating for initial contractionary effects.[8] But balancing the budget by 2002 will be more difficult than envisaged at the time the goals were formulated, given that growth is slower than anticipated earlier. Other factors add to the fiscal risk. Smaller than expected revenue gains associated with the tax increases legislated in 2000 cannot be excluded. Also, there is a risk that sales of housing credits and the shifting of certain operations from the budgets of the states into the enterprise sector might not conform with the principles laid down in the European System of National Accounting. While sizeable savings can be expected from further reductions in government employment in 2001 and 2002 there is a risk that wage increases in the public sector after 2002 might turn out higher than budgeted. Moreover, important parts of the envisaged administrative reform have not yet been designed, and it is unclear whether associated savings will meet expectations in the short term. Pension reform has not yet been completed, and savings implied by the step already implemented in October 2000 might be smaller than expected (see below). There are also risks that currency re-valuations increase the level of the federal government's debt denominated in foreign currency, causing debt-servicing obligations to increase. While this risk materialised recently, when the yen appreciated against the euro, it is also conceivable that exchange rate movements generate budgetary savings. Overall, eliminating the general government deficit in a sustainable way will require strict implementation of planned consolidation measures and prudent budgetary principles. The latter should also include revisiting the cross-financing of certain tasks out of off-budget funds. In the longer term creating a general government surplus would help to cope with fiscal pressures associated with ageing.

The two earlier episodes of fiscal consolidation in Austria in the 1990s both were succeeded by rapidly rising structural deficits thereafter, which did not occur in the EU as a whole (Figure 9). This reflects the fact that previous consolidation policies relied to a large extent on one-off measures rather than structural policies that would have implied lasting consolidation gains.[9] Moreover, with fiscal balances improving new social entitlement programmes were installed. Both of these features are also present in the current consolidation phase. As has been outlined above, one-off measures account for a significant share of the savings generated by the 2001/02 consolidation package. Anchoring general government finances below the deficit line therefore requires fast replacement of the one-off measures by structural reform policies that are associated with lasting savings as intended. Furthermore, the introduction of new family benefits will place a heavy burden on general government finances, amounting more than 0.3 per cent of GDP annually on current estimates. The total costs might even be higher, given that the benefits are likely to reduce labour force participation (see Chapter III below). This reinforces the need to combine spending restraint with structural reform. The

Figure 9. **Fiscal consolidation patterns**
Per cent of GDP

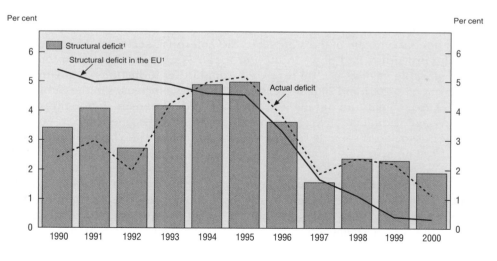

1. As a percentage of potential GDP.
Source: OECD.

government should resist demands to boost entitlement spending further. Instead, social benefits need to be tighter targeted and programmes streamlined. Otherwise there is a risk that budgetary consolidation will be followed by a renewed spending cycle.

The tax raising measures of the savings package are at variance with the medium-term goal of reducing the revenue-to-GDP ratio of the general government, which is high by international comparison. Over the next years tax reductions should be implemented, and these should be connected with measures designed to improve the structure of taxation. In general, a reform strategy that aims at reducing tax rates and broadening the tax base has been found beneficial within the OECD.[10] An option would also be to reduce income taxes at the expense of higher property taxes, which are low in Austria in comparison to other OECD countries.[11] Indeed, tax reductions in 2003 are presently under discussion in Austria. However, despite the fact that tax reductions might be partially self-financing due to positive incentive effects, taxes should only be lowered if substantial lasting expenditure reductions have been implemented. Otherwise current consolidation gains would be put at risk. Moreover, if such expenditure cuts were missing, tax reductions might be perceived by the private sector as a continuation of the fiscal stop-and-go policy, and such adverse confidence effects could reduce the effectiveness of tax reform.

Issues in public sector reform

To a large extent the government relies on pension reform and administrative reform as key elements in its strategy to consolidate general government finances, increase the efficiency of the public sector and widen the scope of market-determined outcomes. Indeed, the size of the government sector in Austria – as measured by general government expenditures to GDP – is large by international comparison: Within the OECD Austria has the fifth highest expenditure ratio. To a considerable degree this is attributable to the level of social spending, notably in terms of outlays for pensions. While the size of a country's government sector is largely a matter of social choice, inefficiencies in public sector operations weigh more heavily the larger the size of government (Figure 10). This part of the chapter highlights important issues in public-sector reform.

Pensions

In the OECD Austria belongs to the countries with the highest public spending on pensions, totalling some 10½ per cent of GDP net of pensions for civil servants, and some 14½ per cent of GDP with the scheme for civil servants added on. The rapid rise in the share of old people in the population expected over the next four decades will insure that Austria will experience a sizeable further increase in pension outlays over the next few decades to come. The old-age

Figure 10. **Government spending by size and economic category**

In selected OECD countries[1]

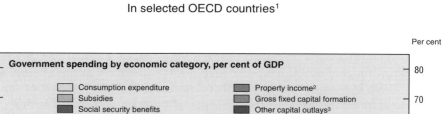

1. In 2000.
2. Including interest payments.
3. Increase in stocks, purchases of land and intangible assets (net) and capital transfers to other sectors.
Source: OECD, *National Accounts.*

dependency ratio – defined as the ratio of persons aged 65 and older to those aged between 20 and 64 – will rise from 25 per cent at present to 53 per cent in 2040, with substantial hikes setting in the middle of this decade according to recent population projections by the Central Statistical Office (Figure 11, panel A).[12] Recognising the threat of demographic developments to the fiscal sustainability of the public pension system, consecutive governments implemented important pension reforms in 1993, 1997 and again in 2000. But these reforms remain partial, and without further policy action Austria's public pension system will require significant increases in pension contribution rates, with corresponding effects on labour costs.[13]

Pension contribution rates presently total 22.8 per cent of the taxable wage base (up from 17 per cent at the beginning of the 1970s), while transfers from the federal budget to the pension system declined over the last decade, and now

Figure 11.   **Projected evolution of the old-age dependency ratio and pension expenditures**

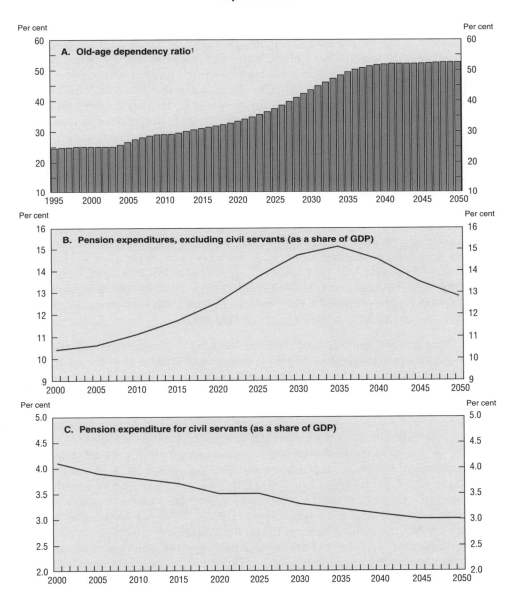

1. Number of persons aged 65 and over as a percentage of number of persons aged between 20 and 64 years.
Source: Statistics Austria; Austrian government and OECD.

amount to some 2½ per cent of GDP. Low effective entry ages into retirement have been identified as a major factor putting the system under stress. In 1999 average entry ages into old-age retirement were 60½ years for males and 58 years for females, which are among the lowest levels within the OECD. Since 1970 the average retirement age for males and females dropped by 3½ years. Earlier reforms merely achieved a stabilisation of the entry age from the mid-1990s on, but did not succeed in increasing it. The measures contained in the 2000 pension reform package aiming at making early retirement less attractive financially and scheduled increases in the minimum early retirement age by 1½ years are therefore welcome steps, although they may not suffice to significantly reverse the trend (Box 2).[14] The recent evolution of early retirements supports the finding – ascertained in previous Austria Surveys – that different early retirement schemes tend to function as substitutes for each other. Old-age early retirement on account of reduced capability to work increased at record rates in 2000 before the scheme was closed in October. Early retirement for the long-term insured and on account of unemployment dropped, with the cumulated decline having reached more than 40 and 30 per cent year-on-year, respectively, by the end of the first half 2001. Simultaneously, however, inflows into invalidity retirement increased markedly, with the accumulated entries having risen by more than 40 per cent year-on-year by the end of the first half 2001. Overall, aggregate inflow into early retirement, including invalidity pensions, has substantially dropped in 2001 compared with the unusually high level in 2000. The decline appears much less pronounced, however, if compared with the preceding years (Figure 12).

The government expects that the 2000 reform measures will generate annual savings increasing from some 0.1 per cent of GDP in 2001 to 0.6 per cent of GDP in 2003 and the years thereafter. Simulations made by the Austrian authorities and submitted to the OECD Secretariat and the EU – incorporating the 2000 reform measures – show pension outlays in the public pay-as-you-go scheme increasing from 10½ per cent of GDP in 2000 to 15 per cent of GDP in 2035. Thereafter, outlays are projected to decline to some 13 per cent of GDP in 2050, as the increase in the old-age dependency ratio levels off (Figure 11, lower panel).[15] If pensions for public employees are added on, projected spending peaks in 2035 at 18 per cent of GDP: Pensions for public employees amounted to 4 per cent of GDP in 2000 and are projected by the Austrian authorities to fall monotonically to 3 per cent of GDP in 2050. While the simulations indicate a substantial deterioration in the fiscal stance of Austria's pension system, the assumed increase in labour force participation appears to be optimistic. Within the next five decades labour force participation is anticipated to increase by around 18 per cent, with an increase of some 33½ and 44 percentage points for males and females, respectively, in the age group of 55-64 years. This would require a sharp decline in early retirements and higher labour force participation of the older people more generally.

Box 2.   **Pension reform 2000**

Major elements of the pension reform that came into effect on 1 October 2000 are:

– The minimum entry age into early retirement on account of unemployment and on a long period of insurance contributions is being increased by a total of 1½ years from October 2000 onwards. The increase takes place in nine equal quarterly steps until October 2002, at two months per step. In the process, the entry age will rise from 55 to 56½ years for women and 60 to 61½ years for males. Similarly, the early retirement age for civil servants will be lifted from 60 to 61½ years for both women and men. There are transitory arrangements for the long-term insured and civil servants.

– The discount of pensions in the case of early retirement is raised up to 3 percentage points annually, up to a maximum of 15 per cent of the pension (18 per cent in the civil service schemes).

– For retirement later than the statutory retirement age (60 years for women, 65 years for men) a bonus is granted of 4 percentage points of the pension base per year.

– Early retirement on account of disability within the old-age pension system has been abolished (in July 2000), following a ruling of the European Court. Simultaneously, eligibility conditions for obtaining an invalidity pension have been relaxed.

– Survivors' pensions in the medium income brackets are being reduced to 40 per cent of the pension of the spouse, from 52 per cent at present. Moreover, an income ceiling has been introduced such that the survivor's pension is gradually withdrawn with total income exceeding the threshold. Survivor pensions' are topped up to up to 60 per cent of the pension of the spouse if the survivor's total income falls short of a certain threshold.

– Annual adjustments of pensions continue to be linked to increases in net wages. If the annual rise in pensions remains below the rate of inflation, compensation will only be in terms of a one-off payment.

Recognising the need for further pension reform, the government has established several expert groups for the purpose of elaborating policy suggestions. Mainly, these concern the harmonisation of the different branches of the public pension system, the introduction of a funded pension pillar, and the strengthening of the link between pension contributions and pension payments. Indeed, the evidence suggests that further reform is necessary, and the agenda of the commissions points in the right direction. However, pre-empting the rapid rise of pension claims over the next years and decades requires early implementation

Figure 12.   **Inflow into early retirement by scheme**[1]

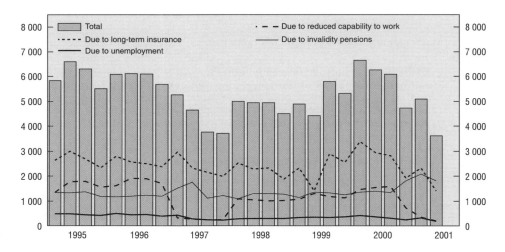

1. Quarterly average.
Source: Austrian government and OECD.

of fundamental reform, rather than piecemeal adjustments that up to now used to be the preferred mode of reform. At present the public pension system splits responsibilities for administering the insurance schemes by various occupational groups. This fragmentation is non-transparent and provides incentives to pressure groups to lobby for more favourable benefits for their respective clientele.[16] The pension system has been found to provide significant incentives for early retirement, and curbing early retirement effectively is likely to require additional measures. In particular, a tightening of eligibility conditions across all types of early retirement is necessary to abolish the substitutability of different channels into early retirement. This implies that eligibility for invalidity pensions should be tightly controlled, based exclusively on health reasons. Also, there should be follow-up checks of health conditions, and re-entry into the labour force should be required if the degree of invalidity improves sufficiently. Standards of this type for invalidity pensions are common in a number of OECD countries. Other channels of effective early retirements outside the sphere of the pension insurance would need to be considered as well, such as extended periods of unemployment benefit receipts with little obligation to actively search for a job (see Chapter III below). Strengthening the link between contributions and benefits received suggests basing pension entitlements to the retirees' earnings base during their entire work history rather than just the best 15 years, as is the case at present.[17] Furthermore, pension benefits that are not linked to earlier contributions by the recipients are best financed out of general tax revenues rather than wage-based contributions. Hence, the redistributive role of the system should be identified, and to the extent such redistribution is not yet covered by budgetary transfers by the government raising the share of tax finance and lowering contributions appears to be warranted.

Benefits provided by the pay-as-you-go part of the system should be adjusted so as to secure the system's fiscal sustainability – notably by correcting the annual adjustment formula for the increase in life expectancy – and a supplementary funded layer developed, and this has been recommended in previous *Surveys*.[18] Such a mixed system has the advantage of diversifying the risks associated with a pay-as-you-go system on the one hand (domestic demographic, political risk) and a funded system on the other hand (capital market risk). Also, this approach would be consistent with the goal of reducing non-wage labour costs to the extent the workers perceive their own contributions as saving rather than tax. Making part of the funded layer obligatory should be considered on fiscal grounds. This could be achieved by transforming the system of severance pay into company-based funded pensions (see Chapter III below). Provisions to introduce a voluntary funded layer into the pension system had already been made in 1999 when private pension investment funds were admitted, which are subsidised by tax concessions. However, despite the preferential tax treatment, the instrument has hardly been accepted by private households.[19] The evolution of such funds should therefore be monitored, and the regulatory framework be reconsidered if necessary.

Health care

The government has continued introducing revenue raising and cost reducing measures in the health care system. Some of the action taken aims at both raising revenues and giving incentives for a more careful utilisation of health care services by consumers. For this purpose, ambulatory co-payments were introduced up to an annual ceiling (€ 73), with exemptions for low-income groups and treatment in special cases such as emergencies, pregnancies and chronic illness. It is still too early for a comprehensive judgement of the effectiveness of this measure, but first outcomes are to be expected at the beginning of 2002. Moreover, co-payments for hospital stays were increased, and prescription fees raised. The degree of redistribution within the health care system was reduced by limiting the automatic co-insurance of spouses of the insured. In the revised system, employees pay 3.4 per cent of their gross wage as health contributions for their dependants, with the major exception of spouses with children or in care. So far, additional revenues generated by this measure have been below expectations. The contribution base was raised by the annual increase in the income ceiling for mandatory health contributions and by extending the obligation to pay contributions to pensioners who receive certain additional pensions.

A high density of beds, care and large equipment in Austrian hospitals accounts for a sizeable share of health care spending. To avoid wasteful replication of such activities and equipment in neighbouring hospitals and overlapping specialisation, the federal authorities and the states have agreed on a revised hospital and major technical equipment plan (*Österreichischer Krankenanstalten-und Grossgeräteplan*) with a planning horizon until 2005. The plan is expected to lead to a restructuring of hospital activities and to more efficient allocation of the technical equipment. As has been outlined in previous *Surveys*, the introduction of the performance oriented reimbursement system for hospitals in 1997 has reduced incentives, inherent in the previous per-diem reimbursement scheme, to prolong the duration of hospitalisation. Average duration of hospital stays has declined since, and this trend has continued. For stays between one and 28 days the average length of stay declined by about one day within the last five years, to 6.3 days in 2000. Overall, this has contributed to dampening the cost increase in the hospital sector, although draw-backs are apparent: the trend increase in the number of hospitalisations was further reinforced, with growth rates of 3.2 and 1.5 per cent in 1999 and 2000, respectively. This is attributable to a rising share of day admissions, reflecting the fact that hospitals now have an incentive to increase the number of cases they treat rather than the duration of stays. Correcting incentives so as to increase accountability and improve resource allocation remains an issue in the Austrian health care system. In this vein, the reimbursement scheme for day admissions will be reformed in 2002. In the new scheme reimbursement for day care will be increased for cases that typically require such treatment and reduced for cases which do not. The financing arrangements for hospitals illustrate the point that further reform in the health care system more generally can lead to substantial efficiency gains, as has been discussed in the special chapter on health care in the 1997 *Survey* and in subsequent *Economic Reports*. Reimbursement rates for hospitals by the states differ across the nine separate *Länder* funds, and this reflects the fact that hospitals are largely funded on the basis of costs rather than efficiency, despite the fact that information is available that allows rating the efficiency of the hospitals' operations. As mentioned in the last survey, this requires standardisation of the criteria by which hospitals are remunerated so as to reward institutions which make the most efficient use of resources.

Administrative reform

Broad areas of administrative reform envisaged by the government comprise reductions in government employment, reducing the size of administrations and scrutinising the services to be provided by the general government as opposed to non-governmental bodies or private firms. While in some fields policy action has already been taken along these lines, some part of the project has not yet been determined. Apart from budgetary considerations, major goals associated with the initiative are increasing the efficiency of the public sector and widening the scope of market-determined outcomes.

Downsizing government employment is a major element of the reform project. On the federal level employment is envisaged to be reduced by 15 000 full-time equivalents, amounting to roughly 9 per cent of federal employees. Of this total, 11 000 full time equivalents will be cut in a narrow sense while another 4 000 will be moved into units that are spun-off from the federal budget as public corporations. All staff reductions are envisaged to be proportionate across the administration with each minister deciding on the allocation of cuts in his domain. In combination with assumed moderate wage increases these measures are scheduled to generate some 70 per cent of cumulated savings in the federal budget this year and next. Staff levels at universities and schools – for which the states are responsible while the staff is largely funded by the federal government – are not directly affected by this policy. However, in these fields measures are planned to be adopted (such as modified regulations for overtime) that yield analogous savings. With respect to simplifying administrations, the government has decided to close several police stations and to merge courts throughout Austria. Implementation in these fields is still pending, however. A working group, consisting of representatives of the federal government, the *Länder* and the communities, has been commissioned to identify savings potentials in the provision of public sector services. This work is still under progress. Another working group, the Task Reform Commission (*Aufgabenreformkommission*) published in March 2001 a list of proposals of government services that could be out-sourced from the private sector or whose provision by the government might be ceased entirely. So far, policy initiatives have hardly been based on these suggestions. In May 2000, new legislation came into force allocating federal ownerships in the postal and telecommunication sectors under the roof of Austria's public sector industrial holding (ÖIAG). The ÖIAG was commissioned to sell a large share of federally-owned entities over the next couple of years, according to a pre-specified plan. Substantial privatisations followed, comprising *inter alia* almost 30 per cent of *Austria Telekom* and all federal shares in *Austria Tabak*. Although in some cases shares were sold to other public sector owners, the programme marks significant progress in Austria's privatisation policies. Also, in October 2000 the government decided on a list of 30 entities within the federal administration to be spun-off until the end of 2003 from the government sector into the public enterprise sector.

Preceding the scheduled spin-offs there have been massive shifts of governmental units into the enterprise sector over the 1990s. Such shifts occurred at all levels of government and are admissible in terms of national accounting if at least half of the revenues of the unit derives from outside (non-governmental) sources. In part, such spin-offs have been motivated by their potential to ease the budgetary burden of the government and to reduce the level of government employment. Moreover, the objective has been to improve the operation of business-like units which could be run more efficiently if made independent of administrative restrictions inherent in a bureaucratic civil service and the governmental budget process.

While transferring units into the enterprise sector can be beneficial on these grounds, attainment of budgetary targets for a few years is not sufficient evidence for economic success. First, there might be opportunity costs in terms of alternative policies that are preferable but are not being pursued due to a lack of comprehensive *ex ante* and *ex post* evaluation concepts. Second, to the extent public sector corporations operate in non-contested markets pressure might be low to base operations and the pricing of services on efficiency grounds.[20] Moreover, budgetary burdens for the government might simply be shifted into the future such that present budgetary relief would be associated with higher financial pressure in the future and the overall discounted impact on budgetary positions might even be negative. As has been outlined in previous *Economic Surveys of Austria*, there is a danger that fiscal discipline of the public sector as a whole might suffer from shifting entities off-budget.[21] Indeed, corporatising government units reduces the associated debt within the general government sector (in the definition of the Maastricht treaty) at the expense of increasing it by the same amount in the sector of public enterprises leaving debt levels of the entire public sector unchanged. To the extent the government ultimately guarantees the financial liabilities of its corporations the government's financial obligations are not reduced.[22] However, the fiscal stance of the government sector is becoming less transparent in that the debt servicing obligations are no longer reflected in general government debt levels, and information on guarantees extended by the various governments to secure the borrowing of public sector companies is not always readily accessible. In a similar vein, spin-offs can be associated with lasting transfers from the government sector to incorporated public sector companies, whose size might not have been anticipated due to insufficient *ex ante* evaluation of likely future cost and revenue developments.

Evidence on the economic success of shifting government units into the enterprise sector appears to be mixed in Austria. Based on evaluations of several spin-offs implemented in the 1990's the Austrian Court of Auditors points to several procedural shortcomings hampering the success of the operations.[23] In the view of the Auditors, past spin-offs have been made without investigating whether the range of services provided by the public sector should be slimmed. The Auditors also note that in some cases the goals of the spin-offs have not been clearly defined – impeding later evaluation – or were not realistic; alternative concepts of incorporation have not been investigated; and concepts of how to generate efficiency gains have not been prepared. One of the deficiencies most frequently spotted was the lack of appropriate analysis of associated costs and benefits in project selection. While the auditors point to several factors that should be associ-ated with efficiency gains, such as a higher degree of cost transparency and more flexible employment conditions within the corporations, they also note that in some cases reduced budgetary outlays for personnel was associated with higher outlays in operating expenses. In contrast, the Austrian Financing Guarantee Asso-ciation (*Finanzierungs-Garantie-Gesellschaft*, FGG), which has also evaluated several spin-offs by the federal government, arrives at a more favourable judgement of the process, which it considers to be successful overall. The FGG concludes that in most cases strategic and organisational targets of the government were attained, and that the government's budgetary targets were either reached or that no dete-rioration in budgetary burdens could be ascertained. The spectrum of services provided widened, while charges increased due to improved quality and more realistic cost accounting. On the other hand, the FGG also notes that the prospects of attaining the objectives of spin-offs has only partially been documented, and that formalised *ex post* control by the government administration in view of stated objectives is largely missing. Also, some corporations – less than half of the cases considered – do not dispose of elaborated and quantitative corporate concepts.[24] Some case studies on the effectiveness of spin-offs have also been made by the Federal Workers' Chamber (*Arbeiterkammer*, AK). The AK notes that evaluation of a broad range of projects has not been feasible due to a lack of pertinent informa-tion. Severe data limitations are also noted for the cases studied, and these con-cern the availability of both economic indicators and the concepts underlying the spin-offs as well as corporate concepts after completion. Overall, the spin-offs are seen as having reduced the budgetary burden for the government, but not in all cases was it considered clear whether the relief would be sustainable. In general, incorporation has been found to be associated with efficiency gains.[25]

Overall, separating government units from the budget can be no substi-tute for more fundamental public sector reform. Choices need to be made what services can be provided by the private sector rather than the government, and to what extent it is appropriate to involve the private sector in the provision of ser-vices provided by the public sector. The proposals that have been made in spring 2001 by the Task Commission, *Aufgabenreformkommission*, constitute a base for reconsidering public sector tasks along these lines and should be utilised accord-ingly.[26] Within such a framework corporatising tasks previously provided by the government can be an important ingredient for later privatisation.

Moreover, to enhance project selection by policy makers an effective framework for *ex ante* and *ex post* evaluation needs to be established. The informa-tion base for policy choices should be improved by systematic use of cost-benefit analysis. For this purpose, it is important to create an accounting framework that reveals the likely future financial burden for the public sector associated with cer-tain policies over a longer-term horizon. Basically, this requires estimating the flows of future revenues and expenditures that accrue up to the termination of a project or over a time horizon extending over several decades. The policy costs are then measured by the present value of these flows, discounted with a relevant interest rate. Assessment of the long-term costs of policy choices for the purpose of improving the allocation of public sector resources is gaining importance within the OECD, and are applied by the United States and – more recently – Japan. The same framework is applicable for *ex ante* evaluation of potential spin-offs from government budgets. In this case, the present value of the difference in projected revenues and expenditures denotes the expected financial burden for the government associated with the public corporation. *ex ante* cost-benefit analysis of alternative projects needs to be supplemented by *ex post* evaluation of actions taken, using an accounting framework for costs and returns that is common across the different types of policies. The fact that the success of separating government units from the budget has been judged quite differently by different bodies points to the scope for ambiguities if such a framework is missing. Progress has been made in recent years in Austria to induce units of the federal administration to apply some form of *ex post* evaluation of their performance. However, for this purpose a large variety of indicators is utilised, varying not only across administrations but also over time. A shortcoming of the present approach is a lack of common benchmark indicators that facilitate comparisons. For effective policy evaluation further action is therefore required.

Inter-governmental revenue sharing

Another issue relating to the efficiency of public sector operations concerns the allocation of tasks and revenues across the different levels of government. Previous Economic Surveys have considered various aspects of allocation mechanisms in place, and in some instances inter-governmental transfer schemes for the purpose of funding specific public sector activities were found to exhibit scope for improvement.[27] Regarding the general system of revenue sharing between the federal government and the state and local governments, new allocations of tax revenues for the different layers of government and of transfers and commissions from the federal government to the states and communities have recently been negotiated, and commitments on budgetary ceilings been made.

Negotiations on revenue sharing between the federal government, the *Länder* and the communities take place every four years. They fix the share of total tax receipts to be allocated to the federal government on the one hand and the *Länder* and municipalities on the other hand, based on anticipated outlays of each layer of government, and specify budgetary targets for each party. The present arrangement was made in October 2000, covering the period between 2001 and 2004. For this horizon the *Länder* agreed to produce annual surpluses of at least 0.75 per cent of GDP (national accounts basis).[28] A temporary shortfall of 0.15·per cent of GDP is allowed if the target is attained on average. Similarly, the local authorities are required to balance their budget, with a transitory under-shoot of 0.1 per cent of GDP being permitted. The federal government needs to restrain its deficit such that the targets for the budget of the general government, laid down in Austria's stability programme, are met. There was also agreement on consolidation measures affecting the federal states, such as spending restraint for personnel of provincial teachers and a relaxation of the earmarking of housing assistance transfers accruing to the states. The shifting of government units into the enterprise sector, in particular hospitals, is also part of the local governments' fiscal programme.

An important issue emerging in the process was how to establish incentives for the states and municipalities to comply with the budgetary limits agreed upon. Eventually, the federal government, the *Länder* and the communities agreed on sanctions in case of a party's non-compliance with the negotiated surplus or deficit. Governments that fail to reach the target on average over the period of the stability pact would have to pay a fixed and a variable fine totalling 8 per cent of the targeted balance and 15 per cent of the shortfall, respectively, up to a ceiling. Sanctions arising from non-compliance with the three per cent deficit ceiling of the Maastricht treaty are also distributed across domestic governments. In each case, however, application of sanctions depends on the unanimous decision of a commission involving the federal government on the one hand, and the *Länder* or the municipalities on the other hand. Also, the agreement specifies circumstances under which targeted government balances need to be renegotiated – such as a significant economic slow-down – and no sanctions apply.

The level of the surplus allocated to the *Länder* and communities for the next four years is broadly in line with budgetary outcomes observed over the last decade. However, the fact that the portion of financial resources accruing to the different layers of government is a matter of negotiation introduces a certain degree of indeterminacy into the allocation of the relative deficits. Different outcomes of the revenue sharing negotiations might simply produce shifts in the relative sizes of budget balances across the levels of government, while the process of negotiating revenue sharing provides few incentives for efficient use of resources and re-evaluations of spending plans. Empirical evidence from elsewhere points to the necessity of introducing incentive-compatible revenue sharing systems. Systems that largely offset changes in local governments' own revenues by changes in shared revenues have been found to provide disincentives to local governments for developing their tax base.[29] There is also a lack of transparency. Increasing public sector efficiency therefore suggests establishing a more incentive-compatible revenue allocation system. General tax receipts should be distributed across government levels in accordance with fixed principles, and the revenue raising powers of the *Länder* and communities should be exercised and extended if necessary. At present, the states and communities finance only a small – and declining – portion of their spending out of revenues exclusively accruing to them (some 8 per cent), and the legislative power for such taxes accrues almost exclusively to the federal government. Indeed, the issue of penalising the *Länder* and municipalities for violation of budget caps argues for the introduction of an incentive system that allows a certain amount of budgetary autonomy of these layers of government – in terms of both spending and revenue powers. Moreover, the congruence between spending and funding needs to be improved. Ongoing policy initiatives that aim at improving the assignment of tasks by government level should thus be combined with budgetary reform along these lines.

III. Implementing structural reform: a review of progress

Previous Surveys have recognised that the Austrian labour market is relatively well functioning, exhibiting a comparatively low level of unemployment and a high degree of aggregate wage flexibility. Indeed, the relatively moderate wage increases and steady employment growth seen in 2000, at a time of significant oil and import price hikes, validate this finding. On the other hand, labour utilisation of females and older workers has been found low, held down, in particular, by generous early retirement schemes. Previous OECD recommendations have therefore emphasised the need to improving the job generating capacity of the economy, and labour utilisation more generally, by wide-ranging measures designed to facilitate the operation of labour, goods and financial markets and to raise the efficiency of the education system. The need for reform is reinforced by the quick deterioration of Austria's old-age dependency ratio and the opening up of a mismatch between qualifications demanded and supplied. Furthermore, potentially large welfare improvements for consumers and contributions to productivity gains warrant further regulatory reform, notably in network industries.

Austria's structural policies continue to be broadly based, largely within the framework of the National Action Plan for Employment (NAP)[30] that covers various policy initiatives not only in the labour market, but also in the education system and product markets for the purpose of fostering employability, entrepreneurship, adaptability and equal opportunities. The new government has particularly emphasised the need to increase incentives in the labour market and effectiveness of job placement to improve the efficiency and reduce the burden of the tax and transfer system, and foster competition in product markets and network industries. Significant policy initiatives have already been implemented or are in preparation. This is true with respect to the pension reform measures, although they cannot prevent a further secular increase in pension contribution rates (see Chapter II above). Measures to reduce non-wage labour costs and improve the targeting of social transfers have also been implemented, notably some tightening of eligibility rules for receipt of unemployment benefits. Moreover, significant steps are under way in regulatory reform, notably in terms of sharpening general competition legislation and stepping up competition in the electricity and gas markets. Despite this progress, in various areas further policy action appears to be warranted and in some fields measures do not appear to be consistent with underlying goals. This chapter highlights important recent developments and reviews the policy measures which have been introduced since the last *Survey*, highlighting fields were the Secretariat would recommend further action. Issues relating to fostering sustainable development are dealt with in more detail in Chapter IV.

Progress in labour market and education reform

Increasing wage and labour cost flexibility

Collective wage outcomes in the past couple of years have been in line with preserving low rates of unemployment, and first steps have been made to introduce a higher degree of wage flexibility on the plant level. In the metal industry a collectively agreed opening clause has been renewed that allows companies to deviate from collectively agreed wages under certain conditions (*Verteilungsoption*). Recent empirical work also hints to a trend towards a larger dispersion of wages across branches. However, no correlation is found between movements in relative wages and in relative employment shares across branches, and this could indicate rigidities in the wage formation process.[31] To the extent sectoral shifts in employment are labour demand induced, they should coincide with relative wage gains in the sectors with increasing employment.

Severance pay

Austria's system of severance pay has come under criticism because of both its negative implications for labour mobility and its non-neutrality with respect to sectoral employment. At present, employees are entitled for severance pay if their employment spell lasted for at least three years without interruption and was not terminated by the employee. Accrual of rights increases in steps with seniority within the company, ranging from two months' salary (after three years of employment) to one year's salary (after 25 years of employment). Severance pay is taxed at a very low rate. For employees this type of severance pay reduces incentives to change employers. The government is now planning to reform the system such that entitlements become portable across employers and commence earlier than presently. Moreover, the instrument shall be transformed into a company based pension scheme with financial support of the government being conditioned accordingly.

Reducing labour mobility via severance pay might be justified to the extent that it allows firms to recover investment in training, which would be lost if the employee quickly changed jobs. However, it is questionable whether the present system of severance pay is an efficient tool for raising the qualification of the labour force, given that entitlements accrue independently of the degree to which the provision of company-based training would be optimal and of the costs for employers associated with such training.[32] Similarly, for low-qualified jobs the system provides an incentive for employers in favour of an early termination of employment spells so as to avoid accumulating severance pay claims that are not matched by productivity gains. Indeed, empirical research indicates that the propensity of employers to terminate employment peaks immediately prior to employment durations that are associated with discretionary hikes in accumulated claims for severance pay.[33] Moreover, the present form of severance pay is systematically biased against labour supply in sectors that are subject to over-proportionate employment fluctuations due to structural change or seasonality as in tourism and construction. Seasonal employment patterns, in turn, account for a high share in Austria's employment dynamics.[34] Overall, the system is associated with costs, while its benefits are ambiguous. Abolishing the system in its present form and using it as a base for the introduction of company-based funded pensions would be warranted (see Chapter II above). This would require that rights start to accumulate in an early phase of the employment spell and that portability be introduced.[35] Implied increases in labour cost would reinforce the need to reduce other non-wage labour costs. But a trade-off between pension accruals and current wages paid would also have to be incorporated into wage contracts, and this might include revisions of wage profiles with respect to seniority. Extending company based pension schemes would also allow for collective contracts that could reduce transaction costs in comparison to individual contracts.

Increasing working time flexibility

In some sectors collective agreements between the social partners have widened the scope for shifting work over a pre-assigned period. The collective contract for the IT and the telecommunication sectors allow flexible working time allocations over a period of one and three years, respectively. For the purpose of lengthening the employment period in the winter in construction flexible working time arrangements based on collective contracts are in force since 1997. The evidence suggests that these arrangements have been effective in reducing seasonal unemployment. Collective contracts for the purpose of lengthening employment periods are now being extended to other sectors that are subject to seasonal variations in employment. Notably this is the case for tourism where an arrangement has been made.

Part-time employment and training leave

Part-time employment has continued its trend increase, with its share in overall employment having risen from 16.8 per cent in 1999 to 17 per cent in 2000.[36]

While this development is broadly based across several sectors, it is particularly pronounced for the service sector, notably in retailing, enterprise-related and financial services, health care and tourism. Similar trends in favour of part-time employment are also observable in other OECD economies.[37] The growing importance of part-time and related forms of employment in Austria is also apparent from the fact that small hours jobs (*geringfügige Beschäftigung*) and work commissioned by firms from self-employed (*freie Dienstverträge*) expanded vigorously in recent years, although the social security tax advantage associated with such jobs relative to regular employment has been reduced. Until the end of 1997 both small-hours jobs and commissioned self-employment were largely exempted from the obligation to pay social security contributions, but since then employers are subject to contributions. While the expansion of small-hours jobs decelerated sharply in 1998, following the introduction of the social security charges, it quickly recovered thereafter (Figure 13).[38]

In 2000 legislation came into force which financially supports working time reductions from full-time to part-time employment of older employees by subsidising compensation of those claiming part-time work (*Altersteilzeit*). Initially, the provision required new hirings for working time reductions to be financially supported. While utilisation of this instrument has been low prior to the revision, take-up rates have significantly increased since. In combination with more restric-

Figure 13. **Small employment and commissioned self-employment**

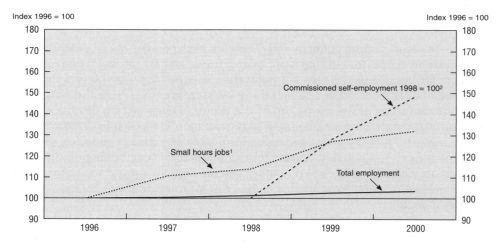

1. Data prior to 1996 are not available.
2. Data prior to 1998 are not available.
Source: Austrian government and OECD.

tive conditions for early retirement (see Chapter II above), this instrument is intended to increase financial incentives for older people to stay in the labour force. It is questionable, however, that the measure contributes to reaching this goal in an economically meaningful way. To some degree the financial incentives will induce employees to reduce their working time who otherwise would have preferred working more hours. Hence, there is a risk that subsidised *Altersteilzeit* might even diminish overall labour utilisation of the older people at the expense of a higher tax burden.

Subsidised training leave, designed to foster job sharing and the employability of the workforce, is now no longer available for women after parental leave, following evidence that benefits have been taken up by women for the purpose of effectively lengthening their parental leave rather than improving their skills. This revision is thus likely to improve the targeting of the instrument. There is little evidence, however, that the training leave has led to new hirings, which are required for leaves associated with very general training goals.[39] Outlays for training the older people – for whom preferential support rates supply – would become more economically viable the longer the older people stayed in the labour force. This reinforces the need to abolish disincentives for continued labour force participation. While both the bonus for hiring older people, paid by the labour office, and the malus for making them redundant have been raised, the impact of these measures on employment are not clear.

Reducing the distortions arising from unemployment insurance and related benefits

The social insurance system has contributed to higher non-wage labour costs in Austria, reducing labour demand, while benefits do not always set appropriate incentives for re-employment of the unemployed and labour force participation. Some measures were recently introduced that lower non-wage labour costs. In the health care system, this is true for the abolishment of the spouses' coinsurance for couples without children (see Chapter II above). On the other hand, the regulations for the employers' sick pay for salaried employees have been extended to blue-collar workers. This entails dropping the two-week waiting period and prolonging the duration of sick pay to between six and 12 weeks annually, depending on the workers' seniority. This measure leads to a significant increase in non-wage labour costs although reduced outlays by the workers' health insurance imply lower contributions. Regulations governing the pay for vacation in case of employment termination were simplified and reformed, leading to a substantial reduction in unit labour costs.

Unemployment benefits

There have been a number of changes with respect to the provision of unemployment benefits, most of them aiming at increasing incentives for job search. Major measures, which became effective at the beginning of 2001, have been:

- A single basic replacement rate (55 per cent of former net earnings), with basic income replacement being topped up for low-income groups, replaces the previous system of several income dependent replacement rates (up to a ceiling of 80 per cent of former net earnings). For unemployed younger than 45 years the level of unemployment benefits is now determined by earnings in the last job preceding the unemployment spell, rather than by earnings in a higher paying occupation dating further back.

- A four-week waiting period for receipt of unemployment benefits has been introduced for unemployed who have terminated their employment.

- The minimum employment period for renewing eligibility for unemployment benefits has been extended from 26 weeks to 28 weeks.

- The maximum duration of unemployment benefits has been temporarily extended to 78 weeks for unemployed aged 60 and older (subject to a certain contribution period) for a transition period up to the end of 2003.

Most of these measures should improve incentives for the unemployed of taking up new employment, and are common practice in other OECD countries as well.[40] In sectors subject to seasonal employment patterns, the extension of the minimum employment period required for re-establishing eligibility following unemployment provides incentives for prolonging employment periods by introducing a higher degree of working time flexibility. In contrast, the lengthening of the maximum eligibility period for receiving unemployment benefits – intended to increase labour force participation, in particular for older people – might turn out to be counter-productive for fostering employment. Econometric evidence for Austria indicates a significantly negative effect of extended eligibility periods for unemployment benefits on the transition out of unemployment for the long-term unemployed, both male and female.[41]

The government has also prepared legislation for the purpose of tightening job acceptance criteria for recipients of unemployment benefits. At present a job offer is defined as "acceptable" if the required qualification is in line with "the learned profession" (erlernter Beruf) of the unemployed. On current planning this shall be modified such that jobs be considered acceptable if they do not significantly render more difficult future employment that is in accordance with the learned profession. The planned new provision has been criticised in the public debate as instigating a dequalification process of the unemployed. Indeed, efficient job matches require a correspondence between qualifications demanded and offered. It is not efficient, however, to dismiss as unacceptable job offers that do not strictly match the unemployeds' past qualification profile. This is particu-

larly true for periods of structural change which are characterised by shifts in qualifications required. Moreover, unemployment of extended duration frequently
coincides with a considerable depreciation of skills, while taking up new employment can improve subsequent re-employment chances in internal and external
labour markets. Tightening job acceptance criteria therefore appears warranted
and the tightening should be increased with increasing employment duration.
This would be in line with common practice abroad.[42]

Child benefits

As has been outlined in Chapter II, child benefits will be extended
in 2002. In contrast to the regulation up to now the new programme provides benefits to all parents, independently of whether or not they have worked prior to the
birth of the child. Also, the period has been extended by one year to three years
while earning caps have been raised.[43] On the one hand, raising the earnings
allowance provides an incentive for extending part-time work. But the income
effect associated with the extension of the eligibility period and the waving of the
pre-work requirement for receiving the benefits will tend to reduce labour supply.
The financial burden associated with extending the transfers would also tend to
negatively influence employment. While the net effect of the measure on labour
supply is ambiguous, studies point to the importance of the availability of childcare institutions for parents' labour force participation. Indeed, while subsidising
childcare facilities would also be associated with a positive income effect for parents, it would strengthen the substitution of labour supply for homework. Allocating funds in this field might therefore be a more effective mean of increasing
labour utilisation.

Improving the services of the Labour Office and active labour market measures

Improving the efficiency of job placements

The government is also preparing institutional reform of the Austrian public employment service (AMS). Key points of the envisaged reform are:

- Integration of the activities counselling, job placement provision of
  active labour market measures and provision of unemployment benefits in one hand at the regional level.

- Differentiation of the job searchers into groups of persons that are easily to mediate and those that are difficult to mediate.

- The government also planned the outsourcing of the financing of the
  Labour Market Office from the federal budget. For this purpose the government plans incorporating the AMS and dropping its financing guarantees for the service. Concrete steps are under consideration.

There appears to be scope for efficiency improvements in the system of employment services. While most successful job matches are based on advertisements or other search channels that do not involve mediation agencies, the share of the AMS in successful job matches has been estimated to amount to less than 10 per cent (excluding the utilisation of the AMS' self-servicing facilities). Private job agencies account for a share that is even lower and also appears to be small by international comparison. The latter finding is likely to be related to the fact that private agencies are subject to certain restrictions. Also, empirical research suggests an increasing skill mismatch between the clients of the AMS on the labour demand and supply side. While the heterogeneity of unemployment with respect to skills and occupations has increased over the last years little has changed with respect to the structure of registered vacancies, reflecting the fact that firms use the AMS primarily as a recruitment channel for unskilled labour and skilled workers with apprenticeship training.[44]

The government's plan to integrate the various activities of the Labour Office on the regional branches of the PES is likely to contribute to increasing the effectiveness of the public employment service. Indeed, experience in other OECD countries suggests that the search intensity of the unemployed and the efficiency of the job matching process increases with the interaction between these functions in the placement process.[45] But a better integration of the system should extend beyond the boundaries of the Labour Office. At present unemployment related benefits of potentially unlimited duration are extended by both the Labour Office and local authorities. The former provides means-tested unemployment assistance benefits (Notstandshilfe) for insured persons whose eligibility for unemployment insurance benefits (Arbeitslosengeld) is exhausted. The latter grants means-tested social assistance benefits (Sozialhilfe) that are paid to the unemployed if their income (including unemployment assistance) falls short of some subsistence level. Eligibility and benefit regulations for social assistance differ substantially between the nine states, and this introduces a lack of coherence between the two systems. Moreover, the fact that for a certain subset of the unemployed the financial burden of granting unemployment related benefits is dispersed between the Labour Office and provincial governments implies that at the margin both authorities face reduced incentives for bringing these unemployed into employment. Close co-ordination between the provision of social assistance and job placement agencies is therefore required.

Moreover, in view of the increased heterogeneity of labour demand and supply, the flexibility of effective placement channels should be widened by increasing the scope of private placement agencies. Several regulations specific to private agencies have been found to constitute serious impediments to job mediation.[46] Persons have the right to sue private placement agencies where the job offered does not conform to perceived promises made. On the other hand, private placement agencies have no means to instigate sanctions when unemployed refuse job offers. Revisiting such provisions is likely to foster the efficiency of the placement system overall.

An option for continued reform along these lines for the purpose of increasing the efficiency of employment services more generally would be requiring the delivery of PES services to become contestable in a market environment. The planned incorporation of the AMS could form part of an institutional base that allows developing the system in this direction. Indeed, many countries within the OECD have introduced contestability of some PES functions, notably in the training area. While the degree to which contestability has been introduced varies, Australia has gone furthest by tendering job brokering and reintegration services. In this system public and private service agencies compete under equal terms and payments are made to them on the basis of outcomes with placement premiums increasing with the degree of the placement risk (higher price tag to difficult-to place job seekers). First experience suggests that it is possible to realise substantial efficiency gains by moving in this direction, while much depends on the appropriate design of such systems, which need to preserve the integration of the various employment services.[47]

Active labour market measures

The National Action Plan for Employment (NAP) assigns an important role to active labour market measures (ALMPs) – as opposed to the "passive" provision of unemployment related benefits – for the purpose of raising employability. Consequently, since 1998 the government has increasingly put more emphasise on ALMPs: in 1999 outlays for ALMPs increased by 29½ per cent, remaining roughly constant in 2000 despite higher economic growth. Enterprises and institutions obtain financial support for the purpose of improving the qualification and integration of the unemployed. Unemployed found eligible for participation in active labour market schemes can also obtain financial aid covering expenses for training, commuting and child minding. These programmes are designed to prevent long-term unemployment – defined as unemployment spells exceeding six months or a full year depending on age – and to foster re-integration of persons with particularly unfavourable labour market characteristics. In 2000 participants in active labour marked measures accounted for almost 15 per cent in terms of unemployment (Figure 14). The government now envisages putting more emphasis on training measures – in particular within-company schemes – at the expense of work provision schemes.

To assess the effectiveness of labour market policies with respect to reducing long-term unemployment, the NAP targets reductions of transition rates into long-term unemployment. For 1999 the NAP aimed at reducing the transition rate into spells exceeding one year to 5.8 per cent, from an observed rate of 6.6 per cent in 1998, and for the 2002 the programme envisages that this rate be

Figure 14. **Persons in active labour market measures**

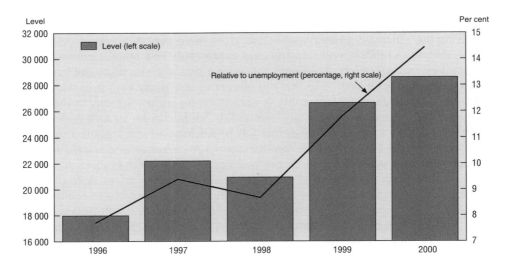

Source: Austrian Institute for Economic Research (WIFO) and OECD.

cut to a half. The actual transition rate undercut the government's target in both 1999 and 2000. However, these outcomes, as well as the over-proportionate drop in long-term unemployment and unemployment of older people, cannot be considered meaningful indicators for the effectiveness of ALMPs. Firstly, movements in the stock and flows of unemployment depend heavily on the evolution of the business cycle and policy instruments such as early retirements. Secondly, any ALMPs of a minimum duration of four weeks necessarily reduce both the length of completed unemployment durations and the stock of the long-term unemployed, even if such measures were not effective at all in improving re-employment prospects. Indeed, in 1999 the observed reductions in transition rates into long-term unemployment are not matched by corresponding increases in transitions into employment (which would also fail to prove the effectiveness of ALMPs). On the contrary, in 1999 exit rates out of unemployment durations of six and 12 months into employment have even declined.[48] Moreover, with respect to the type of ALMPs to be applied these stock and flow indicators provide incentives to expand short-term measures at the expense of measures with longer durations irrespective of their relative effectiveness, because at the same cost the former can be used to interrupt unemployment spells of more people.

Proper evaluation of ALMPs is therefore crucial to determine the intensity and type of their application. Most programme evaluation studies for Austria consider the shares of participants found in employment or not being unemployed following a certain time span after the termination of the measure.[49] The general conclusion is that programme participation is associated with substantial success rates, although some work points to the important role of general labour demand conditions to absorb the unemployed, and work elsewhere suggests that ALMPs might raise the reintegration of participants at the expense of non-participants. Few econometric studies on individual programmes are available, which compare the labour market outcomes of participants in ALMPs with those of non-participants while controlling for heterogeneity in socio-economic characteristics and selectivity in programme participation. Such research is necessary for proper programme evaluation. Indeed, while evaluation studies in OECD countries indicate that active labour market measures can be useful instruments to support job mediation, they produce very mixed results on the effectiveness of ALMPs.[50] Some studies point to participation in work provision and publicly sponsored training measures reducing re-employment prospects rather than increasing them.[51] In particular, standardised work provision and training schemes extended on a large scale and provided outside of companies often do not have a positive impact on transition probabilities into employment. Common other problems include a considerable circularity of the unemployed between different programmes and potentially high crowding out and deadweight costs. Company survey information in Austria on the impact of wage subsidies on hirings also indicates that there might be substantial deadweight costs. In one study some 45 per cent of the sampled firms responded that they would have hired without financial support, and another 15 per cent did not exclude such an effect.[52]

There is some evidence that short spells of training might be helpful to separate those unemployed willing to work from those who are not.[53] Within the OECD, participation requirements in ALMPs are increasingly used as a screening device to arrive at more efficient job placements. In such systems, entitlement for unemployment benefits is frequently reduced if participation is rejected.

Empirical investigations for several countries suggest that for work provision and training schemes to be effective instruments for re-integration they should be tightly targeted in favour of narrowly defined problem groups. The effectiveness of programmes appears to increase the more they are designed so as to address specific unfavourable labour market characteristics of the participants, which reinforces the importance of "profiling" the unemployed with respect to relevant characteristics. Programme efficiency also appears to be related to the degree programmes accommodate demands for training profiles of regional employers. Regional "Alliances for Jobs", as they are increasingly established in Austria, might have a role to play in this respect and should be monitored.[54] A devolution of competencies for designing active labour market policies and channelling participants into ALMPs is also observable in several other OECD coun-tries. Care should be taken, however, that the regionalisation of labour market policies does not lead to a segregation of the different services for the unem-ployed. There is also a risk that financial support for firm-specific training leads to a substitution of labour demand in favour of programme participants that reduces employment chances for non-participants in regional labour markets. Moreover, such measures can be associated with considerable dead weight costs in that they can provide incentives for firms to drop company based training programmes that are not financially supported. These risks reinforce the need to focus more exten-sive work provision and publicly sponsored training schemes on a relatively small group of participants with particularly unfavourable labour market characteristics.

Improving skills and technological know-how

The high importance of skilled human capital within an increasingly "knowledge based" economy underlines the need of revisiting key aspects of Austria's education system, and policy initiatives in this field are being prepared. The government is also preparing legislation to increase immigration to Austria of skilled workers.[55] Indeed, there are already reports that in some fields enterprises find it difficult to fill vacancies for highly qualified labour. A recent study suggests that, under the assumption of a sustainable growth rate of around 2¼ per cent, the mismatch between qualifications demanded and supplied will substantially increase within the next five years.[56]

Vocational training

As has been outlined in previous Surveys, Austria's dual apprenticeship system – which at present absorbs more than 40 per cent of an age cohort after completion of compulsory schooling – has been hitherto successful in providing applied skills, and this has contributed to holding down youth unemployment to comparatively low levels.[57] But previous Surveys have also hinted to the need to broaden the field of application of specific training schemes and introduce new curricula. Since the middle of the 1990s increasing efforts have been made to adapt apprenticeship curricula to new demands, and this policy has continued in 2000 and into 2001. Between 1996 and the beginning of 2001 46 new curricula have been introduced and another 60 have been reshaped, out of 240 vocational curricula at present. The broadening of curricula over the last years included a higher level of general education (particularly in German and foreign languages), and a path was introduced leading to a matriculation qualification for tertiary stud-ies. New vocational training schemes are mainly established for occupations in the service sector and in information technology. Application for training in new fields appears to be high: by spring 2001 50 per cent of all training contracts were in areas which have been either newly introduced or modified. At present policy

makers are shifting their focus from creating new trades to monitoring and supporting the implementation of the newly created or reshaped schemes. In particular, the government is aiming at intensifying the training activities of small and
medium sized enterprises, especially of newly founded enterprises in the services
and IT fields. For this purpose the government is considering to increase financial
incentives for training along with adaptations in legal framework conditions.

The special "rescue network" for youths who do not find training places
has been terminated but was reopened recently in view of deteriorating labour
market conditions. Under this programme financial assistance is given to institutions (which usually do not provide training) to set up ten-month vocational
courses (see the 1999 Survey). Reconsidering this measure appears to be appropriate to the extent the supply of training places offered by private firms improves
relative to demand. Moreover, training in public sector institutions is likely to be
less effective as those within companies.

Non-apprenticeship training within firms might have an important role to
play to upgrade the skills of the workforce within the context of "life-long learn-
ing". While the unions repeatedly demanded educational sabbaticals from work
(one week per year), progress in this field was hampered in that the employers
were not ready to fully finance such sabbaticals, and demanded confining such
spells to those that, in their view, would improve vocational qualifications. At
present the discussion between the social partners has evolved into the direction
of accepting a cost sharing arrangement between the employers and the employees, while establishing decision rules about the choice of admissible training is
still unresolved.

Tertiary education

Since 1993 steps have already been made to increase the effectiveness of
tertiary education. The most significant step was the introduction of Fachhochschulen
(polytechnics), which provide praxis oriented tertiary education in four years studies. The establishments of these institutions turned out to be a success as judged
from both industry's increasing demand for graduates from Fachhochschulen and the
increasing share of students enrolling in these institutions. Efforts have also been
made to increase the degree of autonomy of the universities.[58] Moreover, to support the comparability of Austrian degrees with those granted within the EU,
since 1999 universities have the right to grant bachelor and master degrees.

Nevertheless, Austria's university system has increasingly come under
criticism of being expensive and not well adapting to changing demands for new
skill profiles. Indeed, cumulated costs per tertiary student are the highest within
the OECD, totalling almost twice the mean.[59] Relatively high remuneration for university teachers and long effective durations of studies explain the largest part of
the cost overhang. While the ratio of students to teachers totals about the average,

compensation accounts for 57 per cent of current expenditure as opposed to an OECD average of 46 per cent. Moreover, with 6.4 years the average duration of tertiary education in Austria is the longest within the OECD. At 47 per cent, drop-out rates are also high by international comparison. For example, on an annual basis, spending per tertiary student in Austria is about the same as in the Netherlands. With average duration of tertiary studies being more than one third longer in Austria than in the Netherlands cumulated costs per student exceed the Dutch level by more than 50 per cent (Figure 15). To some extent this finding is attributable to longer statutory study durations due to differences in the degree structure. However, virtual absence of tuition fees and few restrictions on the length students are allowed to spend at universities are further extending effective education periods inducing students to regard universities as a free resource. Moreover, once tenure has been granted there are few incentives for university teachers to deliver adequate teaching and research.

Hence, revisiting the efficiency of the university system should rank high on the policy agenda. It is therefore welcome that the government is preparing legislation to continue university reform. Although certain details are still being elaborated, key features of the planned reform are:

- From autumn 2001 onwards, students will be charged study fees the proceeds of which will be redistributed to the universities. In the present phase of reform the proceeds are planned to be used for investment in the university system.[60]

- Funding of the universities will be based on a contract between the state and the university. Universities will have to introduce a system of cost accounting, and university funding will be subject to performance-related elements. A system of quality control will be established.

- To raise the mobility of staff, contracts for university teachers will no longer entail life long tenure. Moreover, compensation for staff shall contain performance-related elements.

- From 2003 onwards universities will become fully autonomous from the state with respect to setting their agenda of teaching and research. This shall foster developing own profiles of universities. Studies might then be re-allocated to increase cost effectiveness. From this stage on tuition fees will accrue directly to the universities.

Reforms in the product market

Product market reform has continued to progress in Austria. General competition legislation is currently being improved with the planned establishment of an independent competition authority, although its effectiveness may be hampered by insufficient resources and competencies. While regulatory reform in the

Figure 15. **Costs and duration of tertiary studies, 1998**[1, 2]

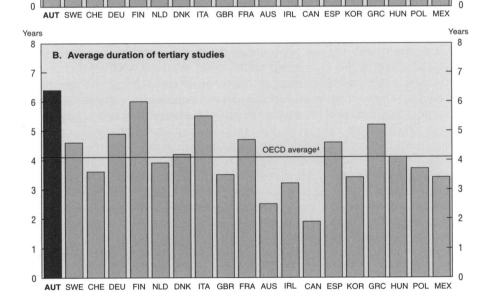

Expenditure (in US$ using PPPs exchange rate)

Expenditure (in US$ using PPPs exchange rate)

A. Cumulative expenditure per student over the average duration of tertiary studies[3]

OECD average[4]

AUT SWE CHE DEU FIN NLD DNK ITA GBR FRA AUS IRL CAN ESP KOR GRC HUN POL MEX

Years

Years

B. Average duration of tertiary studies

OECD average[4]

AUT SWE CHE DEU FIN NLD DNK ITA GBR FRA AUS IRL CAN ESP KOR GRC HUN POL MEX

1. Countries are ranked in descending order of the cumulative expenditure per student.
2. Public and private institutions.
3. Each segment of the bars represents the annual expenditure per student. The number of segments represents the number of years a student stays on average in tertiary education.
4. OECD average: unweighted average.
Source: OECD, *Education at a Glance*, 2001.

telecommunication market started later than in the United Kingdom and the Nordic countries the achievements up to now are significant. The liberalisation of the electricity market – effective since 1 October 2001 – is much more rapid than required by the relevant EU directives, although important issues remain. Similarly, the full opening of the natural gas market, envisaged for autumn 2002, makes Austria one of the first EU countries committed to full liberalisation although important regulatory issues remain. On the other hand, little progress can be observed in other network industries, such as railway and postal services, where only the minimum requirements of the relevant EC directives have been implemented. In other competition related areas, such as more uniform public procurement rules and the extension of shop opening hours, initiatives have been taken, which potentially could enhance the general environment for competition.

The general framework for competition policy

The current regulatory system for general competition issues (particularly mergers and cartels) is based on a cartel court that has limited legal powers to instigate actions independently, but acts on the recommendations of the social partners with the Minister of Economic Affairs and Labour representing the state before the court. In 1998 – in connection with a merger between two of the largest retailers – doubts surfaced concerning the system's ability to enforce competition and its conformity with EU regulations (see OECD *Survey* 1999). A similar situation arose in early 2001 as the final ruling of the cartel court allowed the merger of two of the largest weekly political magazines to proceed, despite the fact that the court's own assessment appeared to suggest the contrary. A major shortcoming of the system is that the involvement of the social partners poses potential conflicts of interest which makes the system vulnerable to pressure from particular interest groups. In both cases mentioned, the parties intending the merger as well as their competitors have been mandatory members of the Chamber of Commerce, which itself is participating in the cartel court proceedings. In summer 2001, the government presented a draft proposal for reform of the Austrian Competition Law. It aims at establishing both an independent Federal Competition Authority acting as an investigator (with a staff of 20-40 persons) and a Cartel Prosecutor, under the Ministry of Justice, with the right to initiate procedure before the Cartel Court. By establishing a Cartel Prosecutor in addition to the independent Competition Authority the government aims at gaining a degree of freedom in initiating competition investigations. The composition of the latter, as well as of the Supreme Cartel Court, will be changed so that judges will have the majority instead of the nominees from the social partners, removing potential risks of interest conflicts. The decisions of the Cartel Court, in turn, can be referred to the Supreme Cartel Court.

Establishing an independent competition authority with investigative powers is an important prerequisite for creating a framework of competition enforcement in line with practices within the EU. However, the creation of two authorities with powers to instigate legal proceedings may lead to a duplication of work and a diffuse allocation of competencies.[61] This, in turn, may jeopardise coherent enforcement of competition regulation and imply unnecessarily high costs, unless a clear separation of responsibilities is put in place.[62] The Competition Authority will have significant investigating powers, including the right to issue information requests and to obtain search warrants from the Cartel Court. The former right is further supported by the possibility to impose sanctions for non-compliance with fines up to € 35 000.[63] On the other hand, the Competition Authority cannot issue administrative fines to companies found to violate the regulations, as is the case in some other EU countries. In contrast, within the framework of sector-specific regulation in the telecommunications and electricity sectors such fines can be issued.[64] In general competition matters the Cartel Court can issue fines of up to 10 per cent of aggregate turnover (as in most other EU countries), reflecting the severity of the infringement. In this context, it is worth noting that experience in other countries points to the importance of fines being sufficiently large to deter anti-competitive behaviour. Moreover, in some countries the effectiveness of cartel prosecution was improved by adopting a "leniency programme" whereby the first firm to divulge the existence of a cartel and to co-operate fully in its prosecution is eligible for reduced sanctions.[65] Although the competition law proposal does not contain an explicit leniency programme, there is a legal provision for the Cartel Court to consider the firms' co-operation in cartel cases when it determines fines. The resources given to the Competition Authority appear to be rather limited. Its staffing appears low by international comparison and compared with the sector-specific regulators in Austria. The Elektrizitäts-Control GmbH and the Rundfunk und Telekom Regulierungs-GmbH (RTR GmbH, former Telekom-Control GmbH) have staff levels of some 50 and 60 persons, respectively. In Denmark, the Netherlands and Sweden the staff of the competition authorities amounts to 90, 170 and 100 persons, respectively. However, differences in staffing levels reflect to some degree differences in competencies, although all three countries have sector-specific regulators as well.

Designing the best framework for promoting and preserving competition involves *inter alia* setting institutional incentives to undertake effective and appropriate regulation. As long as competition in certain market segments has not been established sector-specific regulation is of particular importance. This would favour establishing independent sector-specific regulators, as specific technical in-sight is needed to implement pro-active regulation for the purpose of promoting competition. On the other hand, a competition authority with economy-wide responsibilities is less subject to the risk of "regulatory capture", and may be more willing to eventually phase out regulation in a particular sector.[66] In smaller countries, there might also be a need to concentrate limited resources and expertise within one organisation (see below). All in all, this suggests a continuous adaptation of the regulatory framework to market developments with specific regulation being phased out once competition has been established so as to ensure uniform regulatory treatment of all competition issues.[67] Whichever set of agencies are charged with regulatory functions, it needs to be insured that they are independent of the interests being regulated. Also, as long as regulatory functions are divided between a general competition authority and sector regulators close co-operation between these bodies needs to be ensured.

Energy markets are being liberalised

The Austrian government fully opened the electricity market in October 2001 and is aiming at fully opening the gas market by October 2002. This would imply that Austria is opening up these markets well ahead of most other EU countries. Both network industries are similar in that vertically integrated companies dominate market structures, although the main difference is that the number of parties involved in the gas market is much smaller than in the electricity market and gas – unlike electricity – is mainly imported. Consequently, the regulatory reform considerations are rather similar for the two markets.

Electricity market

The opening of the electricity market was commenced as part of the EU programme for liberalising the European electricity market. Large consumers (with a consumption of more than 20 GWh/year) are already allowed to conclude supply contracts with any electricity supplier, implying that about a third of the electricity delivered to the market comes from a freely chosen supplier.[68] The full opening of the electricity market was completed by 1 October 2001. Given that the EC directive only requires market opening for consumers with an electricity consumption of above 9 GWh by 2003, this places the Austrian liberalisation process well ahead of those in most other EU countries. The opening to competition includes the generation, trade and distribution of electricity, while the transmission is considered a natural monopoly.[69] The consumers' free choice of electricity supplier is technically secured by separating actual consumption of electricity from the supply to the grid.[70] Importantly, this implies that household consumers are not required to install additional measuring equipment, allowing for the cost-free change of supplier and thus enhancing competitive pressure on suppliers.

A considerable degree of vertical integration can still be found in the regional distribution networks – dominated by state and municipal-owned utilities, which generate and distribute electricity as well as being the owner of the local grid.[71] Until October 2001 grid access charges are being proposed by the grid operators on the basis of cost estimates and the Ministry of Economic Affairs and Labour is responsible for approval. In May 2001 the grid charges exhibited a considerable variation, with a 65 per cent difference between the lowest and highest charges (Table 11). This variation partly stems from the guaranteed feed-in-tariffs for promoting electricity generated by renewable energy sources, as grid operators are allowed to recuperate the associated cost through increases in the grid access charge (see Chapter IV for details).[72] However, observed electricity prices vary inversely with the grid charges, such that the variation in the final consumer prices is much smaller and this indicates some cross-subsidisation of electricity, reflecting a monopolistic market structure. Indeed, the difference between the highest and lowest electricity price is more than 200 per cent, which is difficult to explain by differences in technology and the guaranteed feed-in tariffs. Thus, high grid access charges effectively prevent new entry into some of the regional electricity markets, as new entrants would have to charge below-cost prices for electricity to become competitive with the local incumbent. The sector regulator took charge in October 2001. Already earlier, in spring 2001, it announced its intention to reduce grid access charges and narrow their range, and in September the responsible minister reduced the two highest grid charges. A more consistent solution would be for the regulator to use a common framework for determining access charges. More importantly, however, preventing pricing strategies for grid access that do not discriminate against electricity suppliers would require complete unbundling of the existing vertically-integrated utilities into legally independent entities.[73] The present requirement of a mere accounting and management separation does not suffice in this respect.[74]

Table 11.   **Household electricity prices in Austria**
May 2001

Electricity supplier	Grid access charges	Energy price	Total	Total (including electricity levy and VAT) in euro	Electric bill (electricity levy € 0.015/1 000 kWh, 20 per cent VAT) per year, consumption 3 500 kWh
	€/1 000 kWh (excluding taxes, electricity levy)				€
BEWAG (Burgenland)	86	44	129	173	606
Salzburg AG (Salzburg)	92	26	118	159	557
EAG (Upper Austria)	84	31	114	155	542
STEWAG (Styria)	97	15	113	153	536
KELAG (Corinthia)	69	40	109	149	521
TIWAG (Tyrol)	59	50	109	149	521
EVN (Lower Austria)	65	43	108	147	515
Wienstrom (Vienna)	61	41	102	141	493
VKW (Vorarlberg)	64	37	101	140	487
Highest/lowest ratio	1.65	3.28	1.28	1.24	1.24

Note: Ranking of suppliers following the total annual electric bill. Regional discounts are not considered.
Source: Oesterreichische Nationalbank, Elektrizitäts-Control GmGH.

The substantial public ownership of the vertically integrated companies increases the risk of cross-subsidisation from non-competitive to competitive segments of the market. Moreover, privatisation helps establishing the size of stranded costs (costs of non-competitive fixed investment) and shifts the risk of utilities becoming uncompetitive to the private owners. In summer 2001, the EU accepted the Austrian application for financing stranded costs. Between 1999 and the opening of the electricity market, the financial burden of estimated stranded costs for brown coal powered generators was distributed to consumers through an additional € 0.44 per 1 000 kWh surcharge on the electricity price. Since 1 October 2001, with the full opening of the electricity market, the consumers pay a stranded cost fee totalling between € 0.004 and € 0.872 per 1 000 kWh in line with their energy consumption from the national grid company (*Verbundgesellschaft*) in 1997. Indeed, experience in other OECD countries indicates that regulatory reform of the electricity markets in the OECD raises efficiency, but translating this efficiency gain into lower consumer prices depends crucially on the ability of regulatory policies to control market power, further underpinning the need for removing public ownership.[75] An indication of the price reduction potential of the liberalisation of the electricity market can be obtained by comparing electricity prices with those in other EU countries. In mid-2000 the pre-tax electricity price for smaller industrial users in Austria was at least one-third higher than in liberalised markets like Finland, Sweden and the United Kingdom, and for larger household users a similar, although less pronounced, picture emerges (Table 12).

Gas market

The liberalisation of the Austrian gas market is planned to be complete by October 2002 when all consumers will have the free choice of supplier, well ahead of the requirement in the relevant EU directives. Today, the market is characterised by relatively few companies with vertical integration of transmission and distribution of gas (distribution is almost entirely undertaken by the nine *Länder* gas utilities and 16 regional gas utilities) and a substantial share of public ownership. Also, a specific characteristic of the gas market is a prevalence of long-term "take-or-pay" contracts – contracts with gas producers (of which 86 per cent are located in Russia, and the rest mostly in Germany and Norway), obliging the gas importer to pay for the gas regardless of whether it can be sold or not. The liberalisation process has already allowed large consumers (with a consumption of at least 25 million m³ per year, encompassing 24 industrial companies and the gas power stations) to freely choose their supplier, implying that about half of all supplied gas comes from freely chosen suppliers. The scope for reducing prices through a liberalisation of the market is potentially rather large (although less than for electricity prices) as Austrian gas prices, despite being lower than in most countries, are between 10 and 25 per cent above the levels in the countries with more competitive gas markets, such as the United Kingdom (Table 13).

Table 12.   **Electricity prices in EU countries**[1]

Austria = 100

	Industry prices	Consumer prices		
		Level of consumption		
	Small	Small	Medium	Large
Belgium	112.1	129.1	125.3	116.4
Denmark	57.5	132.9	82.6	71.6
Germany	119.1	160.9	130.7	119.2
Greece	74.9	59.8	59.6	66.5
Spain	87.3	93.4	90.9	82.8
France	76.1	108.2	96.5	92.8
Ireland	112.8	116.9	84.1	80.3
Italy	77.5	69.0	167.0	161.1
Luxembourg	106.3	173.7	118.6	107.0
Portugal	94.0	103.4	127.0	111.9
Finland	47.7	100.7	67.3	56.0
Sweden	35.9	135.3	66.3	60.8
United Kingdom	81.4	163.5	92.0	90.3

1.   Without taxes, January 2001.
Source: Eurostat and OECD.

Table 13.   **Natural gas prices in the EU countries**[1]

Austria = 100

	Consumer prices			Industry prices		
	Level of consumption					
	Small	Medium	Large	Small	Medium	Large
Belgium	112.6	107.6	106.9	103.5	118.1	103.8
Denmark	. .	. .	. .	153.8	108.3	89.3
Germany	124.9	115.2	117.7	115.6	137.1	119.3
Spain	111.8	126.0	102.6	86.1	100.2	97.3
France	100.6	96.1	92.5	88.4	107.4	97.0
Ireland	121.5	82.9	. .	83.0	84.1	. .
Italy	92.4	127.0	147.2	113.9	119.0	99.6
Luxembourg	100.6	86.9	99.1	102.5	124.6	119.5
Netherlands	90.4	71.9	76.4	82.0	97.6	. .
Finland	. .	. .	. .	128.4	128.0	86.1
Sweden	91.7	104.0	119.1	145.9	172.3	131.8
United Kingdom	64.7	73.6	79.8	72.6	72.5	65.1

1.   Without taxes, January 2001.
Source: Eurostat and OECD.

As with electricity, the gas market can be separated in areas with little scope for introducing competition, notably (high-pressure) transmission and the (local) distribution of gas, and areas which are potentially competitive like gas supply, gas storage, and gas retailing and marketing.[76] However, the liberalisation law only stipulates separate accounting for transmission, distribution and storage activities within vertically integrated companies, raising similar competition concerns as in the electricity market.[77] The regulatory authority is currently the Ministry of Economic Affairs and Labour, a task which is envisaged to be transferred to an independent authority by October 2002, possibly to the electricity regulator, to exploit synergy effects and available professional knowledge. While this is a very significant step towards opening the market to competition complete unbundling of vertically-integrated companies and withdrawal of public ownership also remain an issue as in the electricity market.

Substantial progress has been made in the telecommunication market

The opening up of the Austrian telecommunication market has progressed rapidly. The number of nation-wide fixed-line telephony providers has increased to more than 30 and since May 2000 there are four mobile phone operators offering their services. Policy actions to promote competition within the telecommunication sector have included the establishment of an independent regulator – the Telekom-Control-Commission and the Telekom-Control GmbH, which later became part of the Regulatory Authority for Broadcasting and Telecommunications (RTR) – the introduction of full number portability (since spring 2000), and carrier pre-selection (since March 2000) for fixed line services.[78] Also, the incumbent (Telekom Austria) was further privatised lowering the government ownership share to below 50 per cent. Consequently, there has been a marked decline in most telecommunication prices. For example charges for fixed line calls are now only a fifth of their level in 1997 with local and long-distance charges converging to the same level. Notwithstanding this progress, prices for a given basket of telecommunication services for both household and business users remain above similar baskets in countries with earlier liberalisation of telecommunication markets, such as Denmark, Sweden and the Netherlands, indicating a scope for further reduction of prices (Figure 16). Interconnection charges fell more than in any other EU country since 1997, and were further adjusted downwards in spring 2001. But they remained above the EU average in 2000 and nearly twice as high as the best practice for local level interconnection.[79] The telecommunication providers are expected to reach a mutual agreement on interconnection charges. Only when this does not materialise the telecommunication regulator will set charges so as to reflect the cost of interconnection, based on a "forward-looking long-run incremental costs model" (FL-LRAIC model).[80] Reductions in interconnection charges could be supported, like in Denmark, by comparison with the best practice in the EU. Charges for local and long-distance calls – particularly during peak time – were

Figure 16. **Telecommunication prices in selected countries**[1]

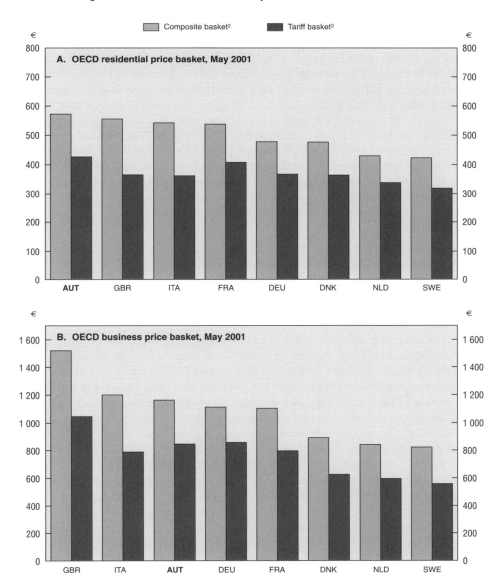

1. Fixed and usage.
2. The composite basket (excluding VAT) includes international calls and calls to mobile networks.
3. The tariff basket (including VAT) does not include international calls and calls to mobile networks.
Source: OECD, *Communications Outlook 2001* and OECD.

higher than in other EU countries in early 2000, although recent policy action may bring these charges down.[81]

The mobile phone market compares well with those of other countries. The market is well developed with high penetration rates.[82] Moreover, usage charges for mobile phones are low in European comparison, although the fixed charges for consumers bring total costs above the EU average.[83] The high penetration can partly be explained by the large subsidies providers have given to handsets. However, number portability is lacking in the mobile phone market and contract periods are long, extending up to one year, and this raises consumers' switching costs thus creating important lock-in effects. The current regulatory framework has been instrumental in developing the mobile phone market, but as the market is maturing competition is likely to benefit from imposing number portability. However, such a pro-active unilateral measure is currently not possible as the regulator is restricted to act on the request of market participants. Thus, an adaptation of the regulatory framework would be required to allow for such pro-active measures.

The prices for calling from a fixed line phone to a mobile phone and "roaming charges" – denoting the interconnection fees charged by foreign service providers for using the mobile phone outside Austria – are substantially higher than the associated costs of providing the services. As in other EU countries, little competitive pressure exists that would lower the cost of calling from a fixed-line phone to a mobile phone as the mobile phone customer is mostly interested in the cost of outgoing calls and the caller has little choice. The cost of calling from the incumbent's fixed-line system to networks of various mobile phone providers may vary up to 33 per cent within the same time band and 60 per cent overall, with the most expensive service being more than four times more expensive than the reverse call for a business user. Regulatory steps have been taken that could lower such prices with the imposition of standard termination and origination fees. In mid-2000 the regulator imposed in steps – within five dispute settlements – fixed fees for termination and origination of calls in the mobile network for all mobile phone service providers (except for a new entrant into the mobile phone market) at the same level, defined by the fees which the provider with SMP (substantial market power) is obliged to apply.[84] This led to fee reductions of more than 50 per cent. However, this decision has been challenged before the Courts. Roaming charges are much higher than domestic calls of similar distance. Regulating such charges is not easy, as it requires the involvement of other countries' regulators, and should not be necessary once competition has broadened sufficiently. In mid-2001 the European Commission began an investigation into possible collusion in the setting of roaming charges by German and English mobile phone providers. A supplementary measure could be to improve information dissipation by publishing roaming charge benchmark tables similar to the EU's present benchmarking of interconnection charges.[85]

Telekom Austria is obliged to provide unbundled access to its local loops and associated facilities with related fees determined on a cost basis by the regulator. Such fees have been reduced by a total of more than 10 per cent in spring 2000 and early 2001. Also, the regulator can impose penalties on the incumbent if it fails to meet the deadlines for providing such access. However, competitors have complained that the incumbent has refused to negotiate with operators not yet granted a license and that the incumbent has discriminated between operators with respect to the provision of collocation facilities.[86] The regulator has gradually reduced the monthly rental fees for leased lines from € 12.35 in 1999 to € 10.90 in 2002. Moreover, growth of the Internet has been rather strong with a penetration rate of 40 per cent by the end of 2000. This development can largely be explained by a relatively high broadband penetration in Austria, which is the fourth highest in the OECD area and the highest in Europe, although it still accounts for a low share of overall network capacity.[87] This, in turn, is related to a widespread availability of cable television networks, which has forced Telekom Austria to quickly upgrade its network to provide digital (DSL) services. The cable television networks also represent a potential for introducing competition between fixed-line networks more generally, although at present only few companies offer network services for voice telephony via the cable TV networks. An additional measure for developing the Internet is the "Signature Act" (effective from 1 January 2000), which created the legal basis for the use of electronic signatures.[88]

Little progress in opening the markets for railway and postal services

Railway services are still mostly provided by the publicly-owned Austrian Rails. In January 2000 an independent regulators were established (*Schienen-Control GmbH* and *Schienen-Control Kommission*) with a similar structure as the electricity regulators, although staffing (six experts and a four-member supervisory board) is considerably smaller. There has been a separation of transport services and infrastructure in accounting terms as stipulated in the relevant EC directive. However, no additional steps have been made to create business identities for each of the two activities, in contrast to several other OECD countries.[89] Indeed, experience suggests that establishing a contestable market for transportation services requires complete separation of the network and transportation services in mutually unrelated companies.[90]

There is also a lack of regulatory progress in the market for postal services. In 1999, the mail and post bus portfolios were split off from telecommunications and incorporated in a separate state-owned company (*Österreichische Post AG*) which has a monopoly for all services related to letters up to 350 grams for the purpose of financing its universal postal service obligation of mail delivery. While the limit of 350 grams is in accordance with EC directives, many EU countries have set lower limits (Germany, Denmark, Spain, the Netherlands, Italy, Sweden and

Finland).[91] Liberalising the market for letters can be expected to generate substantial welfare gains for customers. In contrast, the granting of monopoly rights is no adequate measure to finance universal postal service obligations. The Swedish Post (the former monopolist) regards this obligation as a competitive advantage due to network effects and is not compensated for providing universal services.[92] Even if the costs of providing such services are higher than the value of the competitive advantage, universal services could be commissioned from Austria Post, or any other postal operator, rather than granting a monopoly position on the market for letters.[93]

Public procurement rules

Public procurement rules at the non-federal level of government are not uniform across Austria, except for the cases where the size of the contract requires EU-wide tendering and thus follows EU procurement rules. The differences in public procurement rules may potentially increase administrative costs for bidders and is at variance with ensuring a "level playing field" for competitors. Currently there is a consultative process (expected to be terminated in summer 2002) under way to unify public procurement legislation, and this might lead to an increase in the low share of public procurement effectively open to competition.[94] In addition, a "Federal Procurement Company" was recently established – which administers the largest share of federal procurement – and new administrative measures have been put in place to streamline procedures, such as replacing paper work with electronic information exchange and the Internet publication of all public tenders.[95]

Retail sector regulation

The last extension of *shop opening hours* took place in 1997, allowing shops to remain open a maximum of 66 hours a week between 6 a.m. and 7.30 p.m. every weekday and until 5 p.m. on Saturdays. While the Minister for Economic Affairs and Labour proposed a further liberalisation of shop opening hours, plans for further reform were abandoned due to the opposition of the social partners and the states. A survey carried out by the Chamber of Commerce indicated, however, that the 1997 liberalisation of shop opening hours increased turnover for shops with longer opening hours, significantly raised consumer satisfaction, and had only little effect on employment. Econometric studies elsewhere show positive employment effects of liberalising shop opening hours, and identified Austria as one of the countries in the OECD with the most stringent regulations overall in the retail sector.[96] Thus, deregulation of the sector more generally, including markedly more liberalised shop opening hours, is likely to improve employment creation as well as to increase consumer welfare.

In a similar vein, the rules governing permission to open out-of-town shopping centres (larger than 800 m²) have been eased. This follows complaints about ambiguities of the previous regulation, which required that permits only be given if the local supply of the population with consumer goods and services were not at risk. The precondition is now that the granting of such a permission should not endanger the local population's access for "everyday consumer goods needed at short notice". By ordinance the Ministry of Economic Affairs and Labour has designated that "everyday consumer goods" include foodstuffs as well as detergents, cleansing agents, stationary products and textiles. The local permission process is expected to take between three and six months. Although the new rules appear less restrictive, such regulations also shelter smaller outlets from competition, leading to higher prices and more restricted choice for consumers. To the extent policy makers aim at securing local access to certain types of consumer goods, this could be obtained in an alternative manner – for example by obliging and compensating the retail industry to provide home deliveries – without the need to restrain competition.

Measures to improve entrepreneurship

Some progress has been made in introducing measures to improve the framework for promoting entrepreneurship. The fee for the mandatory membership of Chamber of Commerce has been abolished and founders of new enterprises have become exempted from all taxes and fees in connection with the foundation. The potential personal costs associated with bankruptcy have been lowered. The penalty code has been changed so that debtors can only be charged with gross negligence (punishable with up to two years in prison) in connection with a bankruptcy as compared with the previous stipulation of simple negligence (punishable up to three years in prison). In addition, the list of possible negligence offences has been narrowed down and made exhaustive. On the other hand, the implementation of the one-stop permission process has still not been finalised, although permission procedures should become easier with the planned electronic interchange of documents between the applicants and the authorities involved. This would establish a "virtual" one-stop shop where applicants only have to communicate with one authority, which then co-ordinates the bureaucratic organisation of the permission process.

Financial market developments and regulation

Traditionally, large segments of Austria's financial markets are based on banks offering "universal" services as financial intermediators. Since the EU accession in 1995 the landscape of financial institutions has become more diversified. Several measures have been taken so as to both integrate Austrian financial markets into those of the EU – partly driven by the EU's Financial Services Action Plan – and develop non-banking financial services. In this context special attention has been given to raise the international comparability of financial investment instruments, and to making equity investment more favourable through changes in the tax system. The changing framework for financial regulation includes a unified financial market supervisor authority. The rest of this chapter highlights major developments in financial markets and recent policy initiatives.

Financial market developments

In the mid-1990s, when Austria joined the EU, the volume of investment funds amounted to about one-fifth of the volume of saving deposits. The subsequent quadrupling of assets in investment funds combined with little growth in saving deposits marked a change in the focus of private savings with assets in investment funds reaching three-quarters of the holdings in saving deposits. This coincided with a sharp increase in indirect share ownership, with about one-third of the assets in investment funds invested primarily in foreign equity. Substantial parts of the investment insurance and pension funds are managed by banks and this has led to an adjustment of the banks' income in favour of fees and commissions at the expense of on-balance sheet bank lending. Moreover, the banking sector is subject to ongoing consolidation, involving mergers across the border, while expanding its business to Central and East European countries. At the same time, the central government has sharply reduced its holding of bank shares following the sale of the Austrian Postal Savings Bank in mid-2000. This is an important development towards ensuring a level playing field. At the regional level, the state mortgage banks – fully or majority owned by the *Länder* – pay a commission to the public sector for their guarantees.[97] However, the size of the commissions vary considerably and the relation to the value of the public guarantee is not uniform across banks. In cases where banks have lost their public guarantee their credit rating appears to have worsened, potentially raising refinancing costs.[98] Another factor that may change saving patterns and thus affect the banking industry in the coming years is the abolishment of anonymous bank accounts in November 2000, although the savings behaviour has so far only changed little with total deposits in such accounts remaining at just below 60 per cent of GDP. The identification process of the accounts is still under way with about two-thirds of the holders having been identified by mid-2001.[99]

The Vienna stock market has a very small market capitalisation, equivalent to less than 16 per cent of GDP as compared with an average EU market capitalisation of nearly 110 per cent of GDP. In addition, the part of the shares floating freely totals some 45 per cent, only about two-thirds of the factor in the EU. This makes the market relatively illiquid and reduced the international investors' interest in Austrian stocks. A number of policy measures aim at developing an equity culture and fostering across-the-border capital market integration, as intended in the EU's Financial Services Action Plan. The government's privatisation programme should expand the availability of shares on the stock market, and the sale of a stake of nearly 30 per cent of Telekom Austria in November 2000 was partly directed towards private households.[100] Measures introduced for the purpose of improving the condition for share trading comprise the abolishment of the stock exchange turnover tax in autumn 2000 and the incorporation of the Vienna Stock Exchange as well as a reorganisation of the organised stock market into three separate market segments. In addition, the Vienna Stock Exchange is expanding its international co-operation, having established mutual trading of shares with the *Deutsche Börse* through the XETRA trading system and with the creation in November 2000 of the NEWEX stock exchange for trading of Central and East European shares. Moreover, to enhance investor protection stricter rules concerning equal access to information and the operation of the stock exchange are planned.[101] To further stimulate the international interest in Austrian shares, the Capital Market Promotion Act of 2000 permits Internet publication of prospectuses in English.[102] However, a significant impulse for trading at the Vienna stock exchange did not yet emerge from these initiatives.

A particular concern has been the development of a venture capital market and some success has been achieved in this area with a doubling in 2000 to 84 venture capital firms, although in terms of financing resources the venture capital market remains relatively modest with a combined capital of € 0.2 billion. Most of the venture capital firms are backed by government guarantees and subsidies with, on average, about half of the venture capital coming from the public sector, although recently the private share has increased somewhat. The government-owned *Finanzierungs-Garantiegesellschaft* (FGG) issues capital guarantees of up to 50 per cent for venture capital funds and BÜRGES issues project-related guarantees for private individuals of up to 100 per cent (with an upper ceiling of € 20 000) and for all other capital providers for up to 50 per cent (without any upper ceiling) of the capital invested.[103] Moreover, venture capital funds under certain conditions are subject to preferential tax rules in that individuals are exempted from withholding tax on returns from income invested in such funds (upper limit of € 14 535) and certain funds are exempted from paying corporate income tax. But medium-sized enterprises (SMEs) hardly cover their capital requirement through issuing stocks (a number of IPOs have even taken place abroad) and the Austrian Growth Market, established in 1999 on the Vienna Stock Exchange, to finance SMEs was dissolved in February 2001. Also, low effective taxation of owner-occupied housing is likely to bias investment in favour of real estate.[104]

Financial market supervision is being unified

A new law for a unification of financial market supervision passed Parliament in mid-2001 and will come into force on 1 April 2002.[105] Currently the Ministry of Finance is responsible for supervision of the banking and insurance industries as well as of pension funds – a substantial part of the banking compliance monitoring is carried out by the Austrian Central Bank *Oesterreichische Nationalbank* (OeNB) –

and the Federal Securities Authority (*Bundeswertpapieraufsicht*) is in charge of securities supervision.[106] The supervisory activities concerning banking, insurance and securities are planned to be unified in a Financial Market Supervisory Authority (FMSA), with the operational costs shared by the supervised institutions and – to a lesser extent – the federal government.[107, 108] A number of OECD countries have already established such single supervisory authorities, including Denmark, Hungary, Iceland, Japan, Korea, Norway, Sweden and the United Kingdom.[109] To enhance the enforceability of supervisory measures, the FMSA will be equipped with powers to impose administrative penalties. The unification of financial market supervision might lower the cost of supervision, although this would appear to depend on the integration of existing resources currently employed by theOeNB.[110] However, such an integrated regulatory approach should also be seen in connection with the regulatory challenges presented by the continued integration of financial markets and the emergence of financial conglomerates.

Overview and scope for further action

Since the last *Economic Survey on Austria* there have been a large number of significant policy initiatives – some of which have been implemented and others still being in a preparatory state – that can be expected to improve the functioning of the labour and product markets. The general thrust has been to reduce non-wage labour costs, foster labour force participation, improve the efficiency of job placements and raise the effectiveness of the education system. Furthermore, important progress is being made towards a greater degree of competition in network industries. An overview of the original *Jobs Study* proposals, subsequent developments and recommendations for further action is shown in Box 3.

While several policy measures with respect to the social transfer system are likely to increase work incentives and labour utilisation, important fields remain where further action would be required. In some cases the introduction of new benefit entitlements does not appear to be consistent with the goal of improving the allocative efficiency of labour markets. The following aspects concerning social benefits and the job placement system deserve particular attention to support the ongoing reform process:

- Plans to widen the definition of "acceptable jobs" with respect to the skill profiles for recipients of unemployment related benefits should be implemented. The acceptability criteria should be progressively broadened with unemployment duration.

- The lengthening of the eligibility period for unemployment benefits does not appear to be consistent with other measures designed to improve the incentive structure of unemployment related benefits. Extended durations of unemployment benefits for older people should be abolished. For similar reasons, the difference in replacement ratios

Box 3.   **Implementing the OECD *Jobs Strategy* – an overview of progress**

Since the last review a number of policy measures in the spirit of the OECD Jobs Strategy have been implemented, although in some fields progress has been mixed. This summary reviews progress since the Jobs Strategy recommendations were made for Austria in 1997

Job strategy proposal	Action taken since 1997	OECD assessment/recommendations
I. Increase wage and labour cost flexibility		
• Encourage wage differentiation, greater plant-level bargaining and opening clauses	Greater flexibility agreed by the important metal sector. Changed wage profile for white-collar workers.	Encourage the next step toward genuine opening clauses within the collective bargaining framework.
• Facilitate the employment of older workers and reduce incentives for early retirement	Subsidies introduced for employment of older workers and fines for dismissals. Relaxation of conditions for part-time pensions.	Encourage wage negotiations which seek to take account of the special situation of older workers. As a complement to this reform, make unemployment benefits for older workers more closely follow market wages.
II. Increase working-time flexibility and ease employment security provisions		
• Reform regulations underpinning inflexible working practices	Law governing hours of work liberalised allowing more flexible organisation of working time for industries taking advantage of this (*e.g.* metal). Greater flexibility agreed in some collective contracts.	Review effects of regulations and, when necessary, open possibilities for flexible agreements.
• Liberalise terms for renewing fixed-term contracts	Restrictions reviewed and assessed to require no action.	Keep situation under review.
• Facilitate part-time and casual work	Extension of obligation for employers to pay social security contributions extended to self-employment and to casual jobs. Benefits given to employees for working-time reductions. Subsidised training leave tighter targeted. Restrictions for part-time employment in the public sector eased.	Review the introduction of social security contributions for casual jobs and self-employment with a view to supporting the transition from unemployment to employment. Liberalise restrictions on working time by occupation. Reconsider subsidies for part-time employment of older people.
• Reform dismissal protection	Existing regulations reviewed and assessed to require no action.	Keep situation under review.

Box 3. **Implementing the OECD** *Jobs Strategy* **– an overview of progress** (*cont.*)

Job strategy proposal	Action taken since 1997	OECD assessment/recommendations
III. Reduce the distortions arising from unemployment insurance and related benefits		
• Reduce the incentives for early retirement	Early retirement restricted. Incentives for early retirement pensions reduced.	Consider further means to curb early retirement in the short term and strengthen longer-term measures (stricter eligibility criteria, higher actuarial discounts for pension benefits). Abolish institutional segmentation of pension system. Reduce replacement rates of the pay-as-you-go system. Replace severance pay by company-based funded pensions.
• Reduce unemployment benefits to seasonal workers in the tourist industry	Eligibility conditions tightened.	Monitor and proceed with reforms.
• Reduce disincentives to take up work in social assistance programmes and develop in- work benefits	Unemployment benefits and assistance are now gradually decreased for temporary employment, rather than immediately withdrawn. For unemployment insurance: waiting period introduced, the required minimum employment period lengthened, maximum duration of benefits increased.	To lower marginal effective tax rates at lower income levels, further examine possibilities to raise earnings disregards while simultaneously lowering benefits rapidly as people approach full-time employment. Develop in-work benefits in the context of greater wage differentiation. Widen job acceptance criteria with respect to skills. Abolish extended durations of unemployment benefits for older people.
• Give greater emphasis to active measures and less to passive measures	Subsidies now paid to employers for employing those on unemployment assistance. For those on leave, a subsidy is paid if an unemployed is hired to fill the job or if training is taken up. Subsidies introduced for working time reductions which lead to hirings of unemployed.	Monitor to see whether the restriction to take on unemployed is administratively feasible and that leave is not abused and becomes costly for the economy.

Box 3. **Implementing the OECD *Jobs Strategy* – an overview of progress** (*cont.*)

Job strategy proposal	Action taken since 1997	OECD assessment/recommendations
	Financial aid to firms and the unemployed for training and integrating the unemployed is being expanded. Employment in social and health occupations to be promoted. Subsidies for employment associated with regional infrastructure investment.	Focus the measures narrowly on problem group. Evaluate effectiveness of schemes. Embed support for social and health sector employment in wider reforms which encourage efficiency and sound finance. Ensure efficient infrastructure investment.
		Better integrate the various employment services, including the provision of social assistance. Widen the scope for private placement agencies and introduce contestability of PES-services.

IV. Improve labour force skills

• Preserve and restore the attractiveness of the dual vocational training system, clarify its relationship to higher education.	Curricula for some apprenticeships revised and new occupations introduced. Health insurance contributions for apprentices waived and work hours of apprentices liberalised. Procurement contracts to be linked to training. Tax break granted and injury insurance contribution waived for companies taking on apprentices. Financial assistance to institutions organising additional vocational training.	Continue to revise vocational training curricula and occupations. Avoid attaching subsidies and procurement to training. In support programmes for youths who have not found apprenticeships, ensure that market forces are important in determining the type of training to be offered.
• Shorten and reform higher education and focus it on more occupational-oriented studies. Extend role of new higher level schools (universities for applied sciences)	New university law which allows for shorter study periods. Tuition fees introduced for students.	Shorten higher education and make it more occupationally oriented. Continue with reform of universities. Link funding to performance. Examine potential for moving some study fields to the new institutes of higher education.

V. Enhance creation and diffusion of technological knowhow

• Foster venture capital markets and reduce regulatory barriers	Stock exchange merged with options and futures markets. Vienna exchange now to link with Frankfurt. New single regulator for financial markets. Voluntary take-over code introduced. Programmes to encourage venture capital and business angels.	Lower effective taxation of equity. Widen the potential for investment funds to take equity in enterprises. Focus public financial support programmes on complementing private funding.

Box 3. **Implementing the OECD** *Jobs* **Strategy– an overview of progress** (*cont.*)

Job strategy proposal	Action taken since 1997	OECD assessment/recommendations
• Stimulate the diffusion of technology	Technology package being implemented which seeks to raise level of R&D. Clusters to be promoted in basic research and employment of scientists in industry subsidised. Competence centres being established.	Continue with basic reforms of the university and tertiary sector to encourage greater integration with the economy and increased productivity of research funding.

VI. Support an entrepreneurial climate

• Facilitate the establishment of new enterprises	Regulations governing commencement of a trade liberalised (*Gewerbeordnung*). Relaxed restrictions on opening large-surface shopping centres to protect local shops. Costs of establishing SMEs lowered.	Continue to examine regulatory impediments and improve procedures especially at *Länder* level. Further liberalisation of trades law and of hours of trade.
	Abolishment of stock exchange turnover tax. Establishment of unified financial market supervisor.	Monitor effectiveness of new institutional structure.
• Reform bankruptcy law to facilitate reorganisation	Reform to bankruptcy law, changing governance incentives and powers of individual creditors including a lowering of potential personal costs associated with bankruptcy. Re-organisation procedures established with financial sanctions for directors if bankruptcy follows.	Monitor effects of reorganisation law. Consider extending protection to companies under restructuring. Improve discharge procedures allowing faster re-entry to business life of an entrepreneur.
• Planning approval needs to be simplified	Approval procedures simplified and in some states down to three months.	Monitor the effectiveness of the new procedures and continue reform. Complete the one-shop permission process.

VII. Increasing product market competition

• Encourage competition in the network sectors	Telecommunication liberalisation laws in force. Complete opening of the electricity market by autumn 2001 and of the gas market by autumn 2002.	Adopt a more pro-active policy stance in telecommunication regulation, including full number portability in the mobile phone segment. Monitor telecommunication prices. Continue with energy market reforms and secure complete unbundling of grids from distribution and generation, reinforced by privatisation of utilities. Set access fees in network sectors at competitive levels and insure network access of competitors.

Box 3. **Implementing the OECD** *Jobs Strategy* **– an overview of progress** (*cont.*)

Job strategy proposal	Action taken since 1997	OECD assessment/recommendations
	Accounting separation of railway services and tracks. Establishment of an independent railway regulator.	Establish legal identities for railway services and tracks and ensure non-discriminatory access to tracks for third-party service providers. Reduce the share of letter delivery reserved for the publicly-owned incumbent. Establish an independent regulator.
• Barriers to entry in the provision of local services to be lifted and public and private suppliers placed on an equal basis	No major changes although a number of entities have been taken off budget. Public procurement rules are being reviewed.	Abolish preferential treatment of public suppliers. Introduce greater market testing. Establishing common public procurement rules across different levels of government.
• Pursue privatisation	Postal savings bank (fully) and Telekom Austria (partly) privatised. Creditanstalt privatised. Tobacco monopoly privatised.	Complete the privatisation programme, particularly in liberalised sectors.
• Establish independent competition authority	Proposal to establish an independent competition authority.	Proceed with reform. Secure effectiveness by establishing clear competencies. Monitor if personal endowment is sufficient. Set fines sufficiently high to deter anti-competitive behaviour.

---

between unemployment insurance benefits and unemployment assistance should be reconsidered for the various groups of unemployed persons and widened if necessary.

– Financial support for working time reductions from full-time to part-time employment for older employees (*Altersteilzeit*) do not seem appropriate to increase labour force participation of the older people and should be reconsidered.

– The system of severance pay should be replaced by portable company-based funded pensions.

– The planned increase in child benefits (*Kindergeld*) is likely on balance to reduce working hours supplied by parents. If increasing social support for families is desired, it would be more promising to allocate funds for the purpose of extending child care facilities.

Initiatives to better integrate the different functions of the public employment service are welcome. Similarly, the provision of social assistance should be closely co-ordinated with job placement. Moreover, the scope for private placement agencies within an integrated employment service should be widened and contestability of PES services introduced. Active labour market measures play an important role in the government's employment strategy. Within a framework of improving the "profiling" of the unemployed, ALMPs should be better utilised to test the readiness of benefit recipients to take up work. To secure the effectiveness of training and work provision schemes, measures should be tightly targeted on problem groups. In general there is a risk that private sector entrepreneurial activity is crowded out by public work programmes, and deadweight costs are often substantial. Appropriate evaluation of the effectiveness of the measures utilised with respect to increasing employment chances and minimising deadweight and crowding out effects is therefore imperative and should be stepped up. A promising strategy for "activating" unemployment-related benefits and social assistance schemes is to put more emphasis on in-work benefits that ease marginal effective taxation associated with the transition into employment.

The increasing importance of skilled human capital in a "knowledge based society" reinforces the need for reforming Austria's education system. Tertiary education is costly and its allocational efficiency needs to be improved to cope with an opening gap in skills provided and demanded. Plans for university reform go in the right direction and should be carried through. In particular, while the introduction of tuition fees is welcome raising the financial endowment of the universities is not sufficient for improving performance. Rather, it is important that reform quickly moves on implementing a higher degree of competition between universities and establishes a link between the universities' performance and their funding. Financial support to training enterprises must not introduce a bias in favour of certain occupations or sectors. In general, adapting the pay scales for apprentices to secure the viability of training is preferable over public sector financial support.

Product market reform is progressing in Austria, both with respect to improving general competition enforcement as well as introducing a higher degree of competition into network industries. Progress is uneven, however, and important regulatory issues remain.

The present regulatory system for general competition issues depends on the action of particular interest groups and is vulnerable to outside pressure. Against this background, the establishment of an independent competition authority marks important progress towards a system of effective competition enforcement. There is a risk, however, that an unclear division of executive powers between the competition authority and the newly-established prosecutor, and a lack of effective enforcement powers will hamper the effectiveness of the new competition authority. Thus to secure effectiveness the institutional design of competition enforcement needs to be streamlined. In a similar vein, the government should consider endowing the competition authority with the right to issue administrative fines – eventually subject to the final legal rulings – if firms are found to violate the regulations. More generally, fines should be sufficiently large to deter anti-competitive activity. Adopting a "leniency programme" should be considered, whereby the first firm, which provides evidence on the existence of a cartel and fully co-operates with the competition authorities in prosecuting the collusion, would be eligible for reduced sanctions. Also, it needs to be monitored whether the competition authority is not under-staffed, and the endowment with personnel needs to be quickly increased if necessary in order to avoid long decision delays. Also, the transparency of the regulatory framework overall would increase if the institutional structures of the general competition enforcement on the one hand and of sector-specific regulation were better aligned. In the sphere of general competition enforcement this reinforces the suggestion to establish a competition commission endowed with similar powers as the sector-specific commissions – that have already been established in the electricity and telecommunications sectors – rather than introducing the planned cartel prosecutor.

Regulatory reform in network industries can be expected to generate potentially very substantial welfare improvements for consumers and to contribute to increasing productivity growth in the economy. In telecommunication regulatory reform led to sizeable price cuts and a widening range of services. Significant price cuts have also been observed in the electricity sector. The government fully opened the electricity market by 1 October 2001 and has scheduled the full opening of the gas market for 1 October 2002, well ahead of the requirements stipulated in the respective EU directives. In contrast, regulatory reform in the postal sector is not particularly advanced, and little progress has been made in the railways system. International experience suggests that incumbents tend to exploit their market power, thus preventing the evolution of competitive markets. This includes adopting a strategy where obstruction of competition instigates legal action that may be time-consuming. Hence, opening network industries to competition must pay attention to a number of key factors to be successful.[111] Given the overriding importance of ensuring unrestricted access of competitors to the respective network, independence needs to be established of the grid from the service providers. In the same vein, the regulatory system needs to be sufficiently pro-active to ensure that existing incumbents do not follow an entry blocking strategy. Further action is necessary in Austria to firmly establish these principles in the ongoing reform process. Major outstanding issues regarding competition in network industries are:

- In *telecommunications* the regulatory framework should be extended so as to allow pro-active measures of the telecommunications regulator on its own initiative. In the mobile phone market number portability should be imposed. This would reduce the consumers' switching costs and is thus likely to increase competitive pressures in the market for mobile telephony.

– The introduction in the *electricity* and *gas sectors* of freedom for consumers to move between suppliers, scheduled for this year and the next, respectively, denotes a major achievement, but with vertically integrated utilities dominating these markets effective non-discriminatory access to networks is not fully secured. Thus, to strengthen competition in the electricity and gas markets grids need to be completely unbundled from distribution and generation. At the minimum, this requires a separation of networks and generators into different legal entities. This should be reinforced by privatising utilities.

– In the *postal sector* the monopoly rights for letter delivery should soon be reduced and terminated. To the extent universal service obligations in the delivery of mail are associated with additional costs, financing such services by granting monopoly rights is not adequate. In a competitive market, such services could be commissioned by the government and paid for out of the general budget. Opening the postal market to competition should be fostered by transferring the regulatory competence from the Ministry of Transport, Innovation and Technology to a strong independent regulator.

– In the *railway sector* entry of private providers of transportation services should be fostered. This requires, in particular, that independence be established of the grid from the provider of transport services.

Important regulatory issues also arise with respect to non-network sectors. The regulation of shop opening hours should be liberalised further. To level the playing field for competitors in public procurement, the relevant rules should be made uniform across the different layers of government, based on open tendering. Such action, by putting downwards pressure on procured goods prices, would also aid the process of consolidating general government finances. Several measures have been introduced over the past years to strengthen Austria's financial markets. To some extent, this has been a success, reflected in increased product variety, but equity capital financing of companies still plays a relatively small role. Introducing a funded layer into the pension system should aid the further development of equity capital markets, provided the rules defining admissible pension plans are not too restrictive for investing in pension instruments to be attractive. Furthermore, continued privatisation of public sector companies should contribute to increasing the share of stocks in the portfolios of private households. Privatisation should be extended to the remaining state-owned banks at all levels of government, which would contribute to levelling the playing field in the banking sector particularly in the mortgage segment. However, low effective taxation of owner-occupied housing biases investment decisions in favour of real estate, and this should be corrected.

IV. Encouraging environmentally sustainable growth

This chapter examines the policy mix that has been chosen to reach Austria's environmental objectives with a particular emphasis on the use of economic instruments and the incentives associated with environmentally motivated regulations. The topics presented are selective and intended to illustrate main issues and to provide foundations for policy recommendations, aiming at improving the cost-efficiency of environmental policies, *i.e.* reaching the same or higher level of abatement of pollution at a lower cost to society.[112] This emphasis implies that not all environmental policies are evaluated, nor that the chapter is assessing the state of the environment, which is done by the OECD's *Environmental Performance Reviews*.[113]

Environmental protection has a long tradition in Austria and was first mentioned in a legal context in 1969. Since 1984 there is a constitutional law explicitly obliging the various layers of government – the federal government, the *Länder* and the municipalities – to engage in comprehensive environmental protection. The explicit statement of environmental protection as a constitutional goal – "*Staatsziel*" – reflects the high importance Austria attaches to environmental issues. As a result, Austria has formulated ambitious environmental objectives and has in many aspects achieved a high standard for its environment. The population supports ambitious environmental targets and politicians can rely on a broad consensus for an environmental policy characterised by strict environmental legislation in terms of setting standards combined with a considerable amount of environmentally related public expenditures for environmental purposes, while it is rare that more market-based measures are applied. A major concern of Austrian environmental policies is that they have a common goal of reducing CO_2 and other greenhouse gases emissions – although so far policies are unlikely to achieve the ambitious CO_2 reduction targets.

The next section outlines the environmental policy framework in Austria, including the institutional structure of competencies within the Austrian federation with respect to environmental issues as well as the use of evaluation systems. The following section looks into Austria's commitment under the EU burden sharing mechanism for the Kyoto protocol to reduce CO_2 emissions as an example of ambitious targets.[114] However, the applied policy mix to reach this target appears not to be balanced and its discussion dominates much of the space in this chapter. To the extent economic instruments are applied, they are not tightly targeted on environmental outcomes. Much is expected from "command-and-control" measures and from a re-directing of traditional subsidy programs towards environmental objectives, in such areas as in public transport, housing and biomass energy. These themes are recurrent in other areas: water service providers receive large subsidies to finance infrastructure investments, waste disposal is characterised by detailed recycling regulations, and agriculture receives financial support for organic and other environmentally friendly production methods – the former to the extent that in some markets supply exceeds demand. Bureaucratic decision making tends to pre-dominate in this policy mix. Relying more on market determined outcomes, with individual actors having more room to decide how best to achieve an environmental standard, would allow Austria to maintain its favourable balance between economic growth and a clean environment at lower costs.

The federal institutional structure

The main legislative competence with respect to environmental issues within the Austrian federation is concentrated at the federal level, although the *Länder* are responsible for implementation of federal legislation in general as well as regional legislation in some important areas, such as spatial planning and building standards.[115] The *Länder* are financed through a negotiated revenue sharing system and earmarked transfers from the federal government. For instance in the area of housing policies, the individual *Land* is responsible for the design and allocation of housing subsidies (including the recently introduced opportunity to redirect subsidies to energy saving investments) and the federal government provides the financing. EU directives add an additional layer of competencies, having a direct influence on the formulation of environmental policy at the federal level (like the common agricultural policy and the current deregulation of gas and electricity markets) and with the *Länder* being involved in implementation. While potentially allowing for more subsidiarity, this division of responsibilities can lead to an ineffective policy design, as in the case of policies to promote renewable energy sources in a deregulated electricity market through guaranteed feed-in-tariffs. These are implemented across Austria, but with their levels determined by the individual Land, creating complex incentive structures concerning the supply of renewable energy sources, which may go beyond environmentally justified levels (see below).

The protection of the environment – including strategies for sustainability – is the joint responsibility of the federal and *Länder* governments with the National Environmental Plan from 1997 forming the basis for Austrian environmental policy, including policies to reach Austria's CO_2 reduction commitment. In accordance with the national policy, the federal government and each of the Länder are developing their own action programmes, encompassing several policy areas, such as measures to reduce CO_2 emissions through measures to promote renewable energies and improving the thermal efficiency in the housing stock (see below). However, individual policies in these fields are often pursuing multiple objectives, raising the issue of how to balance policies.

Evaluation of new legislative initiatives

Evaluation of specific projects or broader policies in terms of their environmental effects has not been mandatory in the past, although various evaluation and assessments techniques have been gaining ground. Evaluations of individual projects became mandatory with the Federal Act on Environmental Impact Assessment in 1994, amended in 2000 largely to comply with EU legal framework, requiring an assessment of the direct and indirect effects of each investment project on the surrounding environment as well as evaluating alternatives, replacing earlier more ad-hoc cost-benefit analysis of larger – typically infrastructure – projects.[116] Policies are not systematically evaluated in terms of their environmental impact, although environmental policies are assessed in terms of their economic effects at the federal level through a required regulatory impact statement for all bills presented to parliament. These take into account additional costs for public administration, other fiscal costs, the administrative burden for enterprises, direct effects of the bill on employment and external competitiveness, although economy-wide effects are not evaluated. The state of the environment is closely monitored with the Austrian Federal Environment Agency issuing a "State of the Environment Report" every three years (the latest from 2001) and with individual Länder issuing similar reports at regular intervals. Thus, there has been a move towards greater use of evaluation techniques, although formal mandatory quantitative analyses within a common framework are still to emerge.[117] The United States, for example, is using a common evaluation framework in that mandatory Environmental Impact Statements list the environmental consequences of planned federal government policies and investments and the Office of Management and Budget publishes tables showing the monetised costs and benefits of "economically significant" rules.[118] Naturally, such evaluations come with many caveats, but using standard frameworks for evaluating costs and benefits could form a basis for comparing policies and thereby contributing to a more consistent and cost-efficient implementation.

The Austrian civil law plays a limited role in ensuring an even application of environmental legislation and in enforcing the polluters-pay-principle. In certain cases, affected individuals may apply for an injunction even if the polluter is in compliance with the law, although the burden of proof – often considered difficult and costly – lies with the complainant, thus possibly restricting legal action. Furthermore, third parties – *i.e.* citizens or NGOs not directly affected by pollution – cannot take legal action against the polluter, limiting non-involved parties from using the legal system. On the other hand, third-party action can be taken against government agencies for non-enforcement or non-implementation by bringing a liability lawsuit. Even though specific conclusions concerning the appropriate place of the legal system in environmental policies are difficult to draw, the tendency in other countries is that compliance with the law cannot always be used as a defence and that NGOs have generally the right to take polluters to court, indicating greater scope for using the legal system.[119]

The focus on subsidies and regulatory measures, such as command-and-control instruments, leaves enforcement to administrative action and generally does not allow for much individual scope of how to comply with the law. Moreover, firms only face limited cost of polluting as long as they keep their pollution and emissions below the environmental standards.[120] Indeed, firms are not required to compensate for environmental damages as long as standards are met. At the same time, there is limited use of economic instruments or measures providing financial incentives to change environmentally-damaging behaviour. Environmental goals are therefore in some cases introduced without an integrated catalogue of measures to reach them. Furthermore, Austrian fiscal federalist arrangements lead to a low emphasis on efficiency considerations at the implementation level (the *Länder*), since associated fiscal costs are financed by the federation's revenue sharing mechanism, such as in the case of housing subsidies.

Austria's CO_2 reduction target under the Kyoto protocol

Austria has clear quantifiable objectives with respect to green house gas emissions.[121] Under the Kyoto protocol and the related EU's burden sharing mechanism to reduce EU-wide emission of green house gases by 8 per cent Austria has adopted a more ambitious target of reducing CO_2 equivalents – measuring all green house gases in terms of CO_2 – by 13 per cent by 2008-12 relative to the level in 1990.[122] This should be viewed in the light of Austria – with an energy intensity slightly below that of other countries – having a lower than average CO_2 intensity as compared with other OECD countries, to a large part explained by the high share of hydropower in electricity generation (Figure 17). The relatively low CO_2 intensity, however, also implies that abatement costs – the cost of reducing emissions – in Austria would tend to be higher than in other countries, pointing to potentially large benefits from the application of economic instruments including international trading of CO_2 emissions.[123]

By 1999 the CO_2 emissions (measured in CO_2 equivalents) were somewhat higher than in 1990, mostly related to higher energy consumption and despite

Figure 17. **CO$_2$ emissions and total primary energy supply (TPES)**

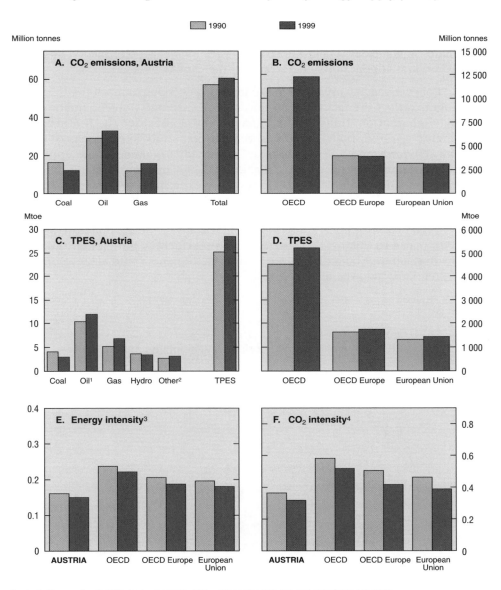

1. Including crude oil, NGL (natural gas liquids), refinery feedstocks and petroleum products.
2. Combustible renewable, waste, electricity and nuclear.
3. TPES divided by GDP (1995 prices using 1995 US$ PPPs).
4. CO$_2$ emissions divided by GDP (1995 prices using 1995 US$ PPPs).
Source: IEA, *Energy Balances of OECD Countries* and *CO$_2$ Emissions from Fuel Combustion.*

some progress in replacing high CO_2 content fuels with natural gas (Figure 18). Extrapolation of historical trends for CO_2 emissions indicates a further modest increase in overall emission by 2008-12.[124] While already implemented measures are expected to reduce CO_2 emissions by as much as 5-6 per cent by 2005, it is unlikely to be sufficient to allow Austria to reach its emission reduction targets. It would therefore appear timely to reconsider the chosen policy.[125]

Policy measures reviewed in the following sections to reach the CO_2 emission targets reflect the fact that two-thirds of all CO_2 emissions originating from electricity generation, transport and space heating. Besides the few economic instruments applied, policies include regulation mainly in the areas of traffic, building standards and heating. Substantial subsidy programmes are applied to promote renewable energy sources, higher efficiency in energy use (in particular for space heating), enhanced efficiency in energy transformation, including co-generation in the industrial and residential sector, and an improvement of transport infrastructures to increase the market share for public transportation. However, the sparse application of cost-benefit analysis means that little attempt has been made to ensure the cost-effectiveness across policies. It therefore appears that a better balance between these instruments could achieve environmental standards at lower costs.

Figure 18. **CO_2 emissions: historical developments and objectives**

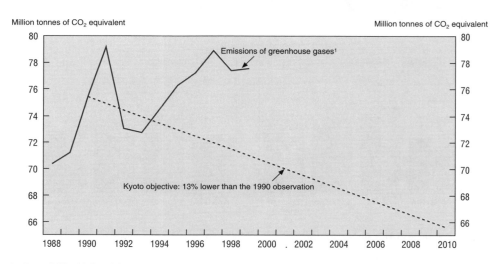

1. Sum of CO_2, N_2O and CH_4 in million tonnes of CO_2 equivalent.
Source: Austrian Federal Environment Agency and OECD.

Economic instruments

Environmental taxes refer in their strictest sense to taxation of each unit of pollution, thereby imposing equal marginal abatement costs across activities as economic agents minimise costs. However, even using a wider definition from the OECD database on environmentally related taxes including all taxes levied on tax bases with a particular relevance for the environment, Austria is relying relatively less on environmental taxes (measured as a share of GDP) than other European OECD countries. Most of those in place predate the debate considering the tax system as a tool to promote environmental goals. Only the energy tax was introduced in 1996, while the introduction of environmentally relevant car characteristics in the calculation of the car registration and operating taxes dates back earlier. Environmental taxes in Austria are largely related to taxation of energy (energy tax imposed on electricity and natural gas and mineral oil tax) and there are significant tax exemptions in place, which are independent of environmental considerations.[126] For competitiveness reasons the energy tax for goods producing firms has been restricted such that tax payments cannot exceed 0.35 per cent of the net production value.[127] This restriction effectively means that a substantial share of all energy consumption faces no incentives from the energy tax to economise on energy. In terms of tax revenues the mineral oil tax is more important with € 2.7 billion.[128] From an environmental point of view the complete tax exemption of coal is rather unfortunate and should, together with all other exemptions, be abolished as exemptions increase the cost of reaching any targeted reduction in CO_2 emissions (see Box 4). More generally, environmental taxes should be geared towards various environmental objectives – such as reducing CO_2 and other emissions – to ensure that marginal abatement costs are equalised across activities.

Private road transport

The general principles behind the Austrian system of vehicle taxation (including road transport duty, vehicle registration tax and motor vehicle taxes) serves to reduce the environmental impact from different types of vehicles, underpinned by strict standards for catalytic converters and petrol quality as well as annual compulsory automobile inspections (including emission controls).[129] The vehicle taxation system of new cars includes a charge based on fuel consumption to promote more energy efficient vehicles as well as a monthly car registration tax dependent on engine specifications.[130] In addition, motorway passes ("vignettes") were introduced in 1997 and their prices were doubled in 2001. Road pricing for goods transport is being implemented in accordance with EU rules, being based on the cost recovery principle, which may include damages to infrastructures but not environmental costs.[131] The current system of road pricing is far from recovering the costs of maintaining the extensive Austrian highway system.

Box 4.   **Competitiveness: a valid reason for sub-optimal
environmental taxation?**

Competitiveness issues have always been a stumbling block to the implementation of a pure CO_2 tax. Indeed, countries applying such a tax (*e.g.* the Nordic
countries and Germany) introduced substantial tax-exemptions from the start to
avoid distorting external competitiveness. The arguments traditionally used
against the unilateral implementation of a CO_2 tax applied to all sectors centre
around the fear of exposing industries subject to international competition to a
loss in external competitiveness in the pursuit of domestic environmental objectives. This would result ultimately in the relocation of workplaces without any global reduction of CO_2 emissions.[1] Consequently, the 1996 Austrian energy tax on
natural gas and electricity introduced rather moderate rates as well as an upper
ceiling of 0.35 per cent of net production value for goods producing firms, and
excludes coal and renewable energy sources altogether.[2]

However, the main purpose of a CO_2 tax is to reduce the activities of the most
polluting industries or make them change their production methods. The loss of
employment (and regional aspects) has to be dealt with in the same manner as
with other structural changes in the economy. Moreover, it is important to recogn-
ise that exemptions for heavy polluters are costly: other domestic industries or
activities are disadvantaged with respect to the protected industry; and overall
costs of dealing with the environmental problem are increased. To reach a given
level of pollution abatement, exempting some activities means that the tax rate or
degree of regulation on others has to be higher, leading to a higher-than-other-
wise contraction of the non-exempted activities, with a likely higher overall loss of
output (given the larger reliance on reducing less pollution-intensive activities)
than compared with a no exemption situation. General equilibrium model numerical simulations indicate that if export orientated sectors are compensated to
maintain their external competitiveness, a CO_2 tax that is 40 per cent higher for a
given CO_2 reduction target is necessary.[3]

For a small and open economy like Austria, there are nevertheless real concerns that some enterprises, if hit by a substantial CO_2 tax, could be bankrupted
or would choose to relocate to another country unnecessarily. The latter refers to
the situation that once other countries also have acted in this field, the operation
of the enterprises in Austria would become viable again. To soften the impact on
external competitiveness and preserve abatement incentives a range of alternative economic instruments could be used. Among the measures applied in OECD
countries are tax credits (as in Sweden for NO_x emissions), reduction of other distorting taxes (such as taxes on labour) or tradable permit schemes (as in the
United States for sulphur and – in some states – NO_x). All these measures reduce
the competitive disadvantage of environmental taxes for large polluters without
diminishing their environmental incentives. An extension of the latter system
could be the creation of an international market for greenhouse gas emission permits, which would reduce the overall costs of meeting the Kyoto target by allowing the emission reductions to take place where abatement costs are lowest.

Box 4.   **Competitiveness: a valid reason for sub-optimal environmental taxation?** (*cont.*)

The design of a CO_2 tax may have different effects on the economy depending on whether the tax is offset by a lowering of payroll taxes, making it revenue neutral.[4,5] However, reducing the marginal abatement incentives for the major offenders on competitiveness grounds is not efficient and is rarely the only means available to reduce adjustment costs.

---

1. It should be remembered, though, that given that relatively limited taxes may have the required effects, the external competitiveness will be influenced by other factors too, such as the exchange rate or the wage rate.

2. Insofar as the energy tax aims at reducing CO_2 emissions, the exemption of renewable energy only reflects that they are CO_2 neutral.

3. In addition, non-linear responses to individual policies could imply that combining polices may have migrating effects on the negative consequences. For example, an increase in the supply of biomass energy could lower the necessary tax to reach a given CO_2 emission target by a third or a half. See Breuss and Steininger (1998).

4. Some calculations have shown that the welfare cost of a CO_2 tax without rebates is much higher than when rebates are made either as a reduction in pay-roll taxes or subsidies to industries. However, these calculations did not include the welfare aspects of expanding the future manoeuvre-room for the fiscal policy. See Farmer and Steininger (1999).

5. Such measures are often assumed complementary in nature, although this may not be the case. For example, an improvement in heating system efficiency would lower the profitability of thermal isolation investments. See Wirl and Infanger (1985) for a more extensive discussion.

The tolled highways are allocated to ASFINAG, a 100 per cent federally owned company, founded in 1997, ensuring that no transfers from the federal government has been necessary since an increase in share capital in 1997.[132] The application of a full cost recovery pricing principle should be introduced to terminate the current environmentally damaging subsidisation of road traffic in Austria. The environmental purposes of the vehicle taxation system are being further impaired by tax-exemptions granted to sectors or vehicle types without obvious beneficial effects on the environment, such as agricultural vehicles, taxis and rental cars. Such exemptions should be abolished altogether.

Minimising the distortion from external effects of road traffic on the environment requires that the marginal cost of car usage is set to be equal with its environmental damages, *e.g.* through instruments like fuel taxes.[133] However, their use has been restricted by the perceived need to set gasoline taxes at levels low enough so as to discourage the so-called "tank tourism".[134] The term refers to the situation where Austrians drive to neighbouring countries with lower gasoline prices to purchase gasoline, which thus lowers revenues without being accompanied by a reduction in emissions.[135] The setting of fuel taxation under the above restrictions has lead to the level being below EU-member neighbours and Switzerland and above those of other non-EU member neighbours (Figure 19).

The lower taxation of diesel than for other fuels (furthered by a fuel consumption levy introduced in 1992 and increased in 1996) has reinforced a trend towards a higher share of diesel-powered vehicles, accounting for two-thirds of new registered cars and more than a third of the stock, leading to a higher share of diesel in road fuels from 36 per cent in the beginning of the 1980s to nearly 60 per cent by the mid-1990s. However, from an environmental perspective taxation of diesel should be higher than that of gasoline as the carbon content is higher in diesel, the emission of NO_x is about a third higher for diesel engines than for non-leaded petrol engines with catalysts.[136] Diesel engines also emit small particles, although volatile organic compounds (VOC) emissions are higher for petrol engines.[137] On the other hand, setting tax rates that fully reflect emissions is difficult as the emissions of small particles – as well as for other important pollutants, such as NO_x and VOCs – are particularly dependent on engine technology and driving conditions.[138] The determination of tax rates for diesel is to a large degree

Figure 19.   **Motor fuel tax rates in European OECD countries**
Q2 2001 or latest available, US$

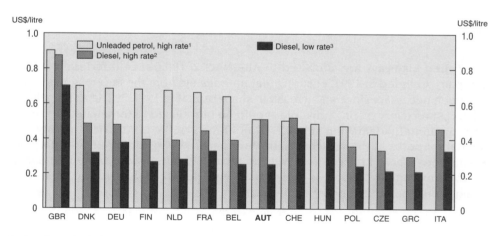

1. Premium unleaded gasoline (98 RON) for households.
2. Automobile diesel for non-commercial use.
3. Automobile diesel for commercial use.
Source: IEA, *Energy Prices and Taxes,* Second quarter 2001.

based on sector considerations. Diesel tax rates are very similar across countries, which may be explained by the trucking industry's use of modern long-distance vehicles, allowing for purchasing of diesel at will along the international route network.[139] However, the current low taxation of transportation fuels in Austria does allow for a higher degree of ecological consideration in the determination of tax rates without having to fear distorting reactions in the form of "tank-tourism".

The present system of energy taxation does serve to reduce CO_2 emissions as a result of the general restraint of demand. However, the costs of abatement are discriminatory as the implicit taxation of CO_2 arising from the current system varies considerably across different types of fuel. In general, the rate on fuels primarily used for transportation purposes is much higher than on fuels primarily used for space heating and usage in industrial production (Table 14). The relative differences, however, do not reflect the content of other pollutants, such as particles or other emissions. Nevertheless, the current energy tax system places a 5 to 10 times higher burden on transport as regards reduction of CO_2 emission as it does on space heating and industrial production, a difference which cannot be explained by the relative content of other pollutants, but may partly reflect other external costs. A re-calibration of taxes in order to reach the Kyoto target should therefore be considered in order to reduce the differences of abatement costs.

While energy taxes are imposing some costs on emissions, only a tax on emissions will minimise abatement costs. Indeed, CO_2 taxes are becoming more widespread in the OECD area, having been introduced in the Scandinavian countries and the Netherlands. Austria should also consider the introduction of a CO_2 tax, which would make the achievement of the intended emission reductions less costly. Insofar as competitiveness considerations complicate the implementation of a CO_2 tax, a cap-and-trade system or tax credits could be introduced to equalise

Table 14.   **Implicit CO_2 tax rates on different types of fuel**

	€/tonne CO_2
Gasoline	127
Diesel oil	85
Gas oil	21
Heavy fuel oil	11
LPG	12
Natural gas	23
Coal	0
Electricity	..

Note: Pre-fund industry for limiting energy tax to 0.35 per cent of value added.
Source: Austrian Government.

marginal abatement costs.[140] Tax credits can mitigate the impact of environmental taxation on rates of return on invested capital. In the Swedish system of NO_x tax credits, applicable to stationary users such as large industrial energy users and power generators, which has a charge on the actual emission, the associated revenue is distributed among the polluters according to the share of energy produced. This ensures net benefits to producers with emissions below the industry average and conversely net costs to those with high emissions. The advantage of this system is that it keeps the incentives at the margin and at the same time avoids a sudden deterioration of profit rates. Alternatively, a cap-and-trade system sets the quantity of allowed emissions and allows for trading afterwards to minimise associated abatement costs. The introduction of such a system with possible grandfathering of permits – i.e. the allocation of permits is related to past emissions – would allow for more equalised abatement costs as well as preserve marginal incentives to abate unlike the current energy tax's upper limit for tax payments. However, both tax credits and cap-and-trade systems are best applicable to large stationary sources of emissions. Mobile sources of some emissions, such as NO_x, are difficult to monitor and measure, making for example catalytic converters the only effective way to reduce NO_x from such sources. Hence, a cost-effective policy to reduce emissions should rely on a general CO_2 tax, but should be combined with regulation to limit some other difficult to measure emissions.

The relatively low CO_2 intensity in Austria indicates that reducing emissions may be possible only at relatively high costs. Therefore the implementation of a CO_2 tax seems particularly worthwhile on efficiency grounds. Indeed, a proposal for such a tax has been evaluated and the results are promising in the sense that environmental objectives could be achieved without disrupting the economy. A macroeconometric evaluation of the tax proposal includes simulations with a lowering of payroll taxes and a time-limited grandfathered tax rebate for energy-intensive sectors as well as subsidies to promote energy efficiency.[141, 142] The study suggests that due to the technological reaction of industry – shifting to less CO_2 intensive production methods – the CO_2 emission reductions would be sufficiently large to meet the government's objective and with only limited overall disruption to economic activity. However, the outputs of export-orientated sectors would decline as they are relatively capital-intensive and will not benefit much from the lower payroll taxes in terms of competitiveness.

Command and control

Environmental regulation plays a central role for vehicles and heating plants. Both standards and control intervals are specified and the recycling of vehicles is regulated. In the case of reducing NO_x emissions regulation is combined with an economic instrument in the form of a higher mineral oil tax. Given the relatively generous conditions for road transport in Austria with relatively low fuel prices and little use of road pricing, it is not surprising that increasing traffic, especially transit traffic, is becoming an environmental problem. Road traffic is a relatively large emitter of CO_2 and it is therefore important to balance policies so as to minimise the associated economic costs. The following section exclusively focuses on mobile emitters, which is not reflecting a valuation of relative importance, but should only serve to outline the principles of the Austrian approach as well as areas where cost-efficiency of policies could be further improved.

Transport and transit traffic

The objectives of Austrian transport policy are to promote environmentally-friendly traffic that fulfils the needs of the economy, taking into account that Austria is a crossroads in Central Europe. In practice this translates into policies aiming at expanding public transportation and transport infrastructures (see below) and, at the same time, minimising the environmental damages resulting from goods (in particular transit) traffic by greater use of rail and waterway transport modes (partly through the promotion of inter-modal co-operation) and regulatory restrictions.[143]

The lower reliance on road transport – as compared with other European countries – makes the modal composition of domestic *freight transport* relatively environmentally friendly with 44 per cent of total tonne kilometre transported by road, 27 per cent by rail, 4 per cent by inland waterways, and 25 per cent by pipeline. One of the environmental problems with freight transport is imported through the transit of goods in the alpine region, concentrating emissions and noise pollution in sensitive and geographically restricted environments.[144] Measures to restrict transit transportation have until now relied primarily on quantitative restrictions. Future policies to restrict transit traffic within the context of a liberalised EU transport market and a projected sharp increase of east-west transit after EU enlargement would have to rely more on economic instruments, such as road pricing (see Box 5). Also emissions from other areas of international transport should be subjected to economic instruments to align incentives with externalities.[145]

Subsidies

The Austrian environmental policy relies more on subsidies and regulatory measures, replacing the role of missing monetary incentives, whereby the non-achievement of an objective is not penalised, but remuneration is offered – in the form of subsidies – to reach a particular objective. In this respect subsidies are often re-directed towards activities with an assumed environmental effect rather than directly on environmental outcomes. The following section provides examples from promotion of biomass and other renewable energy sources, public

Box 5. **Transit traffic**

As part of the EU accession negotiations the "Transit Agreement" – concluded in 1992 – was integrated into the 1994 Treaty of Accession. The agreement regulates overall transit traffic though Austria (as opposed to the EU principle of free flow of transport within the Union) via the so-called eco-point system. The core of the system is that transit journeys through Austria require a number of eco-points – equivalents to the NO_x emission in grams per kWh of the truck. The issuance of eco-points to individual companies is the responsibility of individual countries and mostly based on the grandfathering principle – allocating permits proportionately to the volume of past transits. The determination of the overall level of eco-point issuance per year is set to gradually achieve a reduction of NO_x emission of 60 per cent between 1992 and 2003. The agreement has been extended until the end of 2003. After the termination of the agreement, transit traffic through Austria will be fully liberalised.

In one sense the transit agreement has been successful, as the number of eco-points issued has never been fully utilised and NO_x emissions have been reduced by 50 per cent. Nevertheless, transit traffic has continued to increase in the alpine region. This partly reflects regulatory changes in other alpine countries. However, the use of eco-points has become more concentrated on the alpine transit routes and larger numbers of low-weight trucks (exempted from the eco-point requirement) are being used for transit purposes. In addition, a large part of the transit traffic uses the parallel European Conference of Ministers of Transport (ECMT) permits, which are not subjected to eco-points.[1] The non-tradable ECMT permits provide for multiple entry and multinational transits and were originally issued to facilitate international trade and more recently to ease market integration for new members of ECMT (primarily non-EU countries). The issuance of ECMT permits are designed to stabilise the environmental impact with the number of permits increasing as road hauliers introduce more environmentally friendly vehicles.

The non-economic distribution of eco-points and the absence of a secondary market have prevented a move towards greater use of the cleanest technology available for transit purposes.[2] With eco-points effectively being rewarded through the grandfathering principle, carriers with relatively old and high emitting trucks have been faced with limited restrictions and disincentives to continue operations, particular in the absence of a secondary market for permits.[3] Indeed, if only the newest and cleanest truck technology would have been used in 1996, a 40 per cent reduction in NO_x emissions relative to the base year would have been achieved, equal to about two-third of the targeted reduction. Furthermore, end-of-season shortages of eco-points have enabled some carriers to increase transport prices and thus obtain a private rent on the back of the environmental regulation.

The forthcoming termination of the eco-point system and the failure to reduce traffic in the alpine region requires an alternative system to regulate transit traffic in accordance with EU regulation. The latter implies that the reliance on quantitative restrictions, such as the size of trucks or number of transits, must be abandoned, while bans on night driving for noisy trucks and special speed limits

Box 5.   **Transit traffic** (*cont.*)

for trucks and buses may be maintained.[4] Thus the eco-point system should be replaced by an expansion of existing road pricing schemes to reflect the cost of transit, including environmental costs.[5] However, current EU regulation does not allow for the inclusion of the latter, although a recent white paper [European Transport Policy for 2010: Time to Decide, COM(2001)370] argues in favour of including all external costs in the determination of road charges. Existing road pricing schemes are per transit based and not directly related to the emissions involved. In the future, a new road-pricing scheme could be based on length of transits, specific routes as well as NO_x emissions to take into account local environmental costs – the latter requiring an amendment of the relevant EC directive. The tracking of vehicles and the actual emission could be based on the eco-point system's administrative framework.

1. Puwein (1998).
2. The introduction of tradable emission certificates was proposed by Kerschner and Binder (1998).
3. By 1996, the emission from the most polluting carriers (calculated as the average number of eco-points required from carriers from different nationalities) was around 60 per cent higher than the average off all carriers.
4. Electronic speed limitation was introduced in 1995 onwards with a maximum speed limit for trucks (over 12 tons) of 85 km/h and buses (over 10 tons) of 100 km/h.
5. Since the mid-1990s the Brenner motorway charge has increased from € 36 to € 76 for trucks conforming to minimum noise and emission standards, while other trucks and night runs are charged, respectively, € 101 and € 151. Over the same period annual road use fees have been cut to about a third of their mid-1995 level.

transport, transport infrastructures, and housing for this approach. In general, subsidies are particularly problematic because of their expenditure increasing consequences and are often poorly targeted.

Biomass and other renewable energy sources

A distinctive feature of the Austrian energy supply is a relatively high reliance on renewable energy sources, which is largely explained by the high share of hydropower in the generation of electricity (Figure 20). About two-thirds of potential hydropower capacity have been developed, but further developments are faced with considerable environmentally motivated opposition. With respect to river uses, the Austrian public seems to be more concerned about local environmental goods, like river habitats, and less about the potential benefits of expanding hydropower to affect global warming issues.[146] Despite Austria's ambitious Kyoto target no efforts are being made to improve the acceptability of further

Figure 20. **Renewable energy shares**

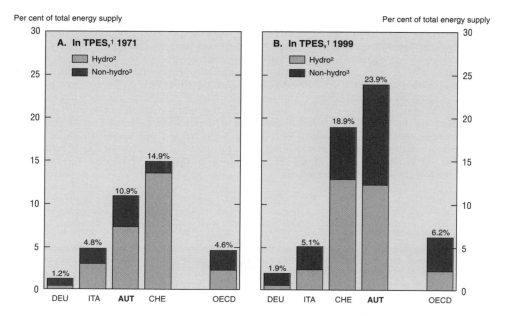

1. Total Primary Energy Supply (TPES) is made up of indigenous production + imports − exports − international marine bunkers +/− stock changes.
2. Hydro shows the energy content of the electricity produced in hydro power plants. Hydro output excludes output from pumped storage plants.
3. Includes combustible renewable and waste (solid biomass and animal products, gas/liquids from biomass, industrial and municipal waste), geothermal, solar, tide and heat pumps.
Source: IEA, Energy Balances of OECD Countries, 2001.

exploiting the local comparative advantages for utilising large hydropower plants. Non-hydro renewable energy sources account for about 1 per cent of the electricity supply and comprises mainly biomass energy and to a lesser degree solar and wind power and heat pumps. In addition, non-hydro renewable energy sources play an important role in the supply of thermal energy.

Despite technological progress, the average production cost of biomass energy is still close to half again higher than that of conventional power stations. Hence, the expansion of biomass as an energy source has taken place on the back of public subsidies which in 2000 covered about one quarter of the total investment of nearly about € 18 million.[147] (Table 15). However, with the forthcoming liberalisation of energy markets in Austria, new instruments to increase the share of renewable energy sources are being introduced.

Table 15.   **Environmentally related subsidies in thousand euro by category, 2000**

Category	No. of projects	Support	Investment	Support share[1] (per cent)
Solar energy	162	1 234	4 321	28.5
Wind energy	7	2 206	33 955	6.4
Biomass – district heating	267	5 108	17 642	28.9
Biogas plant	4	178	739	24.0
Small hydro power stations	39	2 585	10 527	24.5
Heat pump, reclaiming of heat	12	189	668	28.3
Central Heating Plants	8	308	1 099	28.0
Switch to District Heating	73	476	1 746	27.2
Thermal renovation of buildings	37	1 778	6 793	26.1
Energy saving investments of entities	7	366	1 435	25.4
Biomass central heating systems	10	6 194	35 233	17.5
Photovoltaik plants	5	36	120	30.3
Climate relevant investments for reduction of air emissions	2	5 890	48 703	12.0
Biomass rehabilitation investments	27	527	2 341	22.5
Sum of energy		27 075	165 323	
EMAS system campaign	54	893	3 153	28.3
Foundry campaign	1	282	942	29.9
Halon campaign	3	60	301	20.0
Lacquer plant campaign	1	21	103	20.0
Reduction of waste	1	201	573	34.9
Reduction of air pollutants	6	983	7 913	12.4
Total sum		29 515	178 307	

1. Support as a percentage of investment.
Source: Austrian Government.

Electricity and gas markets are being deregulated in line with relevant EC directives. The electricity market was fully opened to competition by autumn 2001 (see Chapter III for a detailed discussion). Currently, the overall electricity supply includes 7½ per cent from small hydropower generators and 1 per cent from generators using other renewable energy sources, mainly biomass. These shares are scheduled to increase to 8 per cent for small hydropower generators by October 2001 (with a capacity of less than 10 MW per year) and in steps to 4 per cent for non-hydro renewable energy sources by 2007. The capacity constraint for small hydropower generators is based on an EU established norm. Keeping in mind the economies of scale in hydropower stations it is not clear why small hydropower stations should be less environmentally damaging than big ones. The share for other renewable energy sources is to be increased to 4 per cent. They include wind power, biogas (mostly from waste dumps), biomass, solar power, and geothermal power. These targets are applicable to each *Land* – limiting the possible exploitation of comparative advantages – although the composition of

non-hydropower renewable energy resources is left to the discretion of the individual Land to allow for a flexible implementation of targets. They will be reached
by imposing obligations on suppliers to expand the supply from small hydropower plants and on grid operators to purchase electricity generated by non-
hydro renewable energy sources, at guaranteed minimum feed-in-tariffs (determined by the Land).[148] The regional distributors – who pay the (above market
rates) guaranteed feed-in-tariffs – are allowed to recover their costs through an
extra grid-charge applicable to all customers (Table 16).[149] To enhance a flexible
implementation of small hydropower plants, a system of "green certificates" for
electricity generated by such plants will be introduced, whereby grid operators
with a production exceeding the target share can sell the surplus of renewable
energy to other operators in the form of "green certificates".[150] In case the stipulated targets are not met, the grid operators must pay a compensation fee into a
fund set up to promote electricity generation by renewable energy sources. However, given that the electricity supply from small hydropower plants is close to its
target, the new support system would appear to mostly preserve their share of
electricity production. In addition, the federal law stipulates that Länder can
impose on grid companies the purchase of electricity from Combined Heat and
Power (CHP) plants with a minimum payment per kWh as long as the CHP plant
also serves the public district heating system, although no numerical targets are in
place.[151] The implicit values of reducing CO_2 emissions through the guaranteed
feed-in-tariffs differ across technologies and between Länder as well as being at
variance with the implied value used in other policy fields. The values attached to
CO_2 reduction are at least about twice the estimated value of CO_2 for trading
under the Kyoto Protocol as estimated by the OECD.[152]

Table 16.   **Survey of guaranteed feed-in-tariffs for electricity generated by renewable
energy sources (summer 2001)**

€/1 000 kWh_el netto	Geothermal electricity		Solid or liquid biomass		Biogas		Landfill gas		Sewage gas		Wind		Photovoltaic	
	Min.	Max.	Min.	Max.	Min.	Max.	Min.	Max.	Min.	Max.	Min.	Max.	Min.	Max.
Burgenland	23	94	23	94	23	94	23	94	23	94	23	65	73	145
Carinthia	0	0	52	174	30	94	34	58	34	58	57	97	545	727
Lower Austria	36	124	36	124	73	94	73	94	73	94	36	89	129	129
Upper Austria	39	93	26	168	26	156	26	81	26	62	26	118	559	653
Salzburg	31	83	31	83	31	83	31	83	31	83	31	83	31	83
Styria	44	99	45	135	45	135	45	135	45	135	53	118	363	363
Tyrol	83	83	55	83	69	83	55	55	55	55	83	83	276	276
Vorarlberg	39	111	38	111	39	111	39	111	39	111	39	111	111	111
Vienna	30	124	30	124	36	92	36	92	36	92	36	85	110	110

Source: *Einspeisungen elektrischer Energie aus erneuerbaren Energieträgern in das öffentliche Netz, E.V.A. (Cerveny, Veigl), 2001.*

While a certain degree of flexibility has been introduced into the system to promote renewable energy sources through individual (*Länder* specific) implementation and green certificate trading, setting targets for renewable energy has an inherently arbitrary element, reflecting the lack of cost-benefit analysis. In addition, the targets are only indirectly related to the environment and with no built in incentives to achieve an equalisation of CO_2 abatement costs. Similar reductions of CO_2 emissions might be obtained in other and potentially cheaper ways, such as replacing the coal powered plants by a less CO_2 intensive energy source. Moreover, the restriction of "green certificate" trading to electricity generated by small-scale hydropower plants does not fully exploit the possible flexibility in such schemes. It should at least be considered to include electricity generated by all forms of renewable energy and preferably to international trading keeping in mind the global focus on CO_2 emission reduction.

The variation in the *Länder*-determined guaranteed feed-in-tariffs means that the incentive structure to promote renewable energy varies considerably across *Länder* as well as across technologies, favouring different types of technologies at different locations without regard to local circumstances. Indeed, the implementation of technologies best adapted to local circumstances can only be realised in a neutral system of guaranteed feed-in-tariffs as such a system will ensure local specialisation according to comparative advantages. Even if the variation in the guaranteed feed-in-tariffs was to reflect other local environmental concerns, then the 100 per cent difference between the highest and lowest feed-in-tariffs for the most common type of renewable energy – biomass – cannot be related to a similar variation in local circumstances. Furthermore, the implicit abatement cost associated with the guaranteed feed-in prices is high. In Lower Austria, the expansion of renewable energy in electricity generation is expected to reduce CO_2 emission by around 55 000 tonnes. The similar amount of emissions allows conventional power plants to produce 60 to 140 GWh (depending on primary fuel and power plant technology). Thus, the implied social abatement costs of promoting biomass energy through guaranteed feed-in tariffs in Lower Austria, measured as the additional cost (the difference between the average feed-in-tariff and the production costs for conventional power plants) range from € 58/tonne of CO_2 – if renewable energy replaces older coal power plants – to € 134/tonne of CO_2 in the case of the most efficient natural gas power plants (Table 17).[153] These estimates do not include public subsidies for the construction of renewable energy power plants. In case the expansion of renewable energy sources is replacing alternative expansions of the electricity supply, probably by modern natural gas power generators, the associated abatement costs appear very high (see the section below concerning thermal efficiency in housing), highlighting the need for cost-benefit analysis in policy selection. Indeed, reserving a share of the electricity supply for biomass generators is rather arbitrary. In addition, financial support to expanding the supply of any type of electricity would in

Table 17.   **Productions costs and feed-in tariffs in Lower Austria**

	Small hydro power plants	Biomass	Biogass	Wind power	Solar power
Production costs €/1 000 kWh	29-102	109	109	73	727
Feed-in tariffs €/1 000 kWh		36-124	73-94	36-89	129
Average		87	87	67	

Source: Government of Lower Austria, OECD.

itself lead to higher energy consumption, unless a similar amount of electricity from other (high emission) energy suppliers is effectively withdrawn from the market. In addition, subsidising renewable energy sources suffers from a bureaucratisation of the technology decision process. An alternative and probably more efficient policy would be to introduce a properly modified CO_2 tax, not taking into account other environmental concerns and competitiveness issues in the electricity generating sector, which leaves the choice of renewable energy technology to the market (see Box 6). The system of guaranteed feed-in-prices has a similar effect to that of taxes on electricity prices insofar as associated costs are passed on to the consumer. Thus, replacing them with a CO_2 tax should not lead to resistance from consumers as well as being a more effective policy.

Public transport

Public transport has, in an international context, a fairly high market share of 20 per cent of all passenger traffic (measured in passenger kilometres), split into 12 per cent for railways and 8 per cent bus transport, enabling road traffic density for passenger transport (relative to available network length and GDP) to remain somewhat below the OECD-Europe average.[154] The perceived beneficial environmental effects of public transport are partly the background – as described below – for substantial investment subsidies to expand the services. However, the environmental impact of specific modes of passenger transport is a function of the primary source of energy, technology, and the average occupancy rate. Public transportation has a relatively small level of emissions as compared with other modes of transportation. Overall CO_2 emission from public transportation (excluding buses) per passenger kilometre is only 10 per cent of the similar concept for cars as a result of the high reliance on electricity and with the railway system even owning hydro-power plants. Occupancy rates for railways are on average rather low, as a result of the public service obligations of providing public transport outside rush hours and in thinly-populated areas, leading revenues to only cover about half of total costs and with the deficit covered by subsidies from the central government. Promoting environmentally friendly public transportation would appear to rest on two issues:

Box 6. Biomass as a renewable energy source

Austria's substantial forestry resources and the relatively low population density in the alpine regions make biomass a natural main plank in the Austrian strategy for developing non-hydro based renewable energy sources. Biomass is considered CO_2 emission neutral as long as the total amount of biomass used in electricity generation is renewed through new biomass growth. Biomass is a generic term for the extraction of energy from a number of sources, ranging from the incineration of straw to exploitation of methane from municipal waste dumps, although the latter is often referred to as biogas. In the Austrian case, the emphasis is on waste products from the forestry sector. At present, however, the biomass technology is not sufficiently developed to produce energy at costs comparable with conventional power generators. Combined with a consideration of the production of biomass incinerators as an infant industry, this has resulted in substantial subsidisation of biomass energy (see above).

Estimates suggest that for biomass technology to become competitive with conventional power generators through the introduction of CO_2 taxation would require CO_2 tax rates of between € 54 to € 73 per tonne of CO_2, implying a tripling or more of the present (implicit) CO_2 tax on energy for power generation (see Table 17).[1] Such energy price increases would probably lead to larger reduction in CO_2 emissions than targeted, both as overall energy demand drops and as demand switches from relatively high carbon content fuels like coal and diesel to relatively less carbon intensive fuels, such as hydropower and natural gas. Moreover, such a CO_2 tax would be at least 50 per cent higher than the estimated price of an internationally traded CO_2 permit.

---

1. Pichl *et al.* (1998).

- The present low CO_2 emission levels for public transportation is largely the result of consumed electricity being generated by the railway sector's own hydropower plants. Thus, insofar as these plants are fully utilised, the expansion of public services will be powered by electricity purchased from a competitive market, where the average CO_2 intensity is higher. Indeed, the use of electricity from its own hydropower plants may in itself – in the absence of price signals in the planning process – lead to a misallocation of electricity, both internally in the railway sector and externally by pre-empting other energy users.

- Increasing rail capacities may not necessarily reduce traffic volumes in other modes, therefore policies should focus first on securing higher occupancy rates, which would appear to depend on making existing public transportation more attractive for users.

Evaluation of current policies in terms of environmental impact is difficult, as no comprehensive statistics of CO_2 emissions for individual public transportation modes are available.[155] The absence of proper cost and price signals makes it is next to impossible to optimise the demand and supply of public transportation with respect to the environment. Local bus transport is exempted from mineral oil tax, implying that the implicit value of emissions set by the government does not enter as a parameter in the provision of public transportation. Moreover, ticket prices are set independently of actual transport costs. Consequently, abatement costs in public transportation are largely unknown, implying that such considerations do not enter planning decisions. Thus, there is room for manoeuvre to further limiting the environmental impact of public transportation simply by improving the planning of public transportation through improving data collection and enhancing the information content in prices by removing tax exemptions and subsidies. However, a fully competitive market for public transportation, including privatisation of public providers, combined with a CO_2 tax would more effectively promote environmental objectives. Public service obligations could be subjected to public tenders (including environmental objectives), thereby introducing a wider choice of technologies. Social concerns should be dealt with by direct means tested benefits to those who are affected by full-cost pricing of transport services, but not by subsidising the service itself.

Transport infrastructures

The Austrian infrastructure is well developed, and road network and railway densities are comparable to most other European countries. In order to reduce the negative environmental effects from the north-south transport patterns, one of the main planks in the Austrian transport policy has been to promote a shift of goods and passenger transport from roads to railways, involving a substantial investment programme in the railway infrastructure. The government has increased available financial resources and reallocation of resources from other infrastructure programmes to finance this expansion. Since 1990, about € 6.5-7.3 billion has been committed to expand railway services (particularly long-distance) and mainly channelled into investments. Apart from environmental considerations, such an expansion was believed to enable a reduction of operating losses, at the time running at around one third of operating costs (excluding imputed interest). Nevertheless the railway system continues to rely on government subsidies (Table 18). As infrastructure investments in the road network were scaled back at the same time the overall thrust of investment was largely concentrated towards railways, despite this sector's shrinking market share of passenger and goods transport. Looking into the future, closer economic integration with the EU accession states (further accelerated in case of an EU-enlargement) point to the need for a further development of road, and to a smaller degree, railway connections to the east.[156]

Table 18.   **Public infrastructure investments**

Million euro

	1992	1993	1994	1995	1996	1997
Railways	1 315	1 459	1 207	922	892	1 074
Roads	1 031	1 042	1 102	985	988	

Source: Bundesministerium für Umwelt, Jugend und Familie (1999), Beschäftigungseffekte umweltrelevanter Verkehrsinvestitionen, Wien.

An expansion of railway infrastructure (mainly by expanding capacity on existing routes) might increase the use of railways and improve cost coverage as the result of network effects similar to those seen in air transport. Part of the railway infrastructure expansion is intended to replace road transport of goods through the alpine regions. An expansion of container terminals could help improving the interaction with other transport modes, although requiring that corresponding investments are undertaken in neighbouring countries. A connected issue is the low and seasonally fluctuating capacity utilisation on parts of the railway infrastructures. The more recent trend to close rarely used tracks with low capacity utilisation should also be welcome from an environmental point of view. Like in other cases, a more comprehensive application of cost-benefit analysis could contribute to a more cost-effective use of available funds to expand transport infrastructures.

Improving the thermal efficiency of the housing stock

The strategy to improve the *thermal efficiency* of the housing stock is pursued through stricter building standards for new construction of buildings and subsidies for thermal efficiency investment and for the expansion of district heating systems. All *Länder* offer subsidies to improve thermal efficiency of the existing housing stock with the federal government funding the various programmes, within a total housing subsidy programme of € 2.5 billion.[157] The subsidies are designed by each *Land* and take the form of cash subsidies (either as a fixed payment or as a share of renovation costs) or as loan support and are granted according to various criteria, although a common overall objective is CO_2 emission reduction. In one of the *Länder* (Vienna), the total expected amount of subsidies for improving the thermal efficiency of the housing stock is expected to amount to € 36 million per year, leading to a projected reduction of CO_2 emissions of 15-20 000 tons per year.[158] Assuming depreciation rates of 1 to 3 per cent, the public cost of reducing CO_2 emissions amounts to – according to Secretariat estimations – between € 80 to € 102 per tonne of CO_2 within a 30-year time horizon.[159] Further studies are needed to identify the appropriate policy mix between setting building standards, subsidisation of thermal insulation investments, and a relaxation of rent controls (allowing landlords to recover the investment costs necessary to improve thermal insulation) in combination with the introduction of a CO_2 tax.

As part of the strategy to reduce CO_2 emissions from housing, *district heating* and *combined heat and power* (CHP) *plants* are being promoted, providing heating for more than 10 per cent of the housing stock and almost half of public buildings.[160] The fairly high connection rate to district heating systems has been stimulated by financial support provided by the federal government and by the Länder (in some cases requiring new houses to be connected) in the form of direct investment support and grants to allow free grid connection for customers.[161] The small-scale district heating systems powered by biomass have been promoted by setting subsidies so that individual heating bills will be no higher than in the case of oil-fired systems.[162] Moreover, heating is cross-subsidised by electricity in the CHPs as the assured minimum price for electricity is sufficient to cover costs, allowing the setting of heating prices below full costs.[163] In addition, there is little effective energy taxation of heating from CHPs. Thus, the combination of free grid connection and low and non-taxed heating expenses has been instrumental in expanding the district heating network, even possibly beyond its optimum.

Agriculture and the environment

Agriculture in Austria is based on a large number of small family owned-farms and with a strong reliance on organic farming.[164] As a consequence Austria has avoided many of the environmental problems often associated with modern large-scale farming, typically in terms of ground and surface water pollution, and functions together with the forestry sector as an important sink of CO_2. On the other hand, maintaining traditional farming in Austria has required government payments (amounting to some € ½ billion) under the Austrian Environmental Programme (ÖPUL) in line with the European Common Agriculture Policy.[165, 166] The predominance on small farms can be seen in connection with perceived external effects as the structure of agriculture is considered important for providing a suitable landscape to attract tourism. Notwithstanding the positive environmental impact of ÖPUL, which is largely brought about by a high participation rate, it could possibly be improved by directly aiming at environmental outcomes (see Box 7).

Public financial support to promote organic farming are provided to about 8½ per cent of all farms, more than in any other EU country and are on average nearly 20 per cent higher than for conventional farms.[167] Organic farming's crop yield is on average a 20-30 per cent lower than compared with conventional farms, while organic animal production has roughly the same yield as

Box 7. **Austrian agriculture and support**

The agricultural programmes to support environmentally sustainable agricultural developments in Austria have been grouped together in the ÖPUL (established in 1995 in connection with the EU accession and renewed in 2000). The aim is to have a broadly based policy encompassing all of Austria (combined with some area specific measures) to protect the environment above prescribed minimum standards and has been instrumental in ensuring that average agricultural incomes have not declined following EU accession. Individual farmers are allowed to chose and combine any of the 34 different individual measures – mostly directed at production methods – independently of the farm's location, with the most popular measures favouring extensive farming (through premiums for reducing the use of fertilisers or reducing land use).[1] Nearly three-quarters of all farms participate in the programme, covering about 90 per cent of the agricultural area.[2] More than two-thirds of all farms are run on a part-time basis, with any landowner of more than ½ hectare land being able to participate in the agri-environmental programme if a set of conditions is fulfilled.

The environmental benefits of the extensive farming methods in Austria can be measured in an internationally low average nitrogen balance of only 29 kg/ha compared with eight times higher levels in the Netherlands, a country with particularly intensive farming. Moreover, the high share of organic farming means that the use of commercial fertilisers is well below the average in the EU and that the general use of pesticides has been reduced – and other active ingredients stabilised – since the programme was introduced. However, the reported low average values reflect large regional variations. Using the broadly based and production method orientated ÖPUL to solve what are basically local problems runs the risk of inadequate targeting and strengthening local considerations might improve cost-effectiveness. An alternative way to solve such problems would be to directly link the policy instrument to the environmental objective, for example by taxation of nutrient surpluses (as in the Netherlands), which requires establishment of farm level nutrient accounts in the affected areas to calculate the nutrient discharge to surface or groundwater.

The distribution of financial support is mostly related to different production methods and takes into account specific environmental objectives only indirectly. Consequently, the ÖPUL serves to maintain particular agricultural technologies, which does not promote new or existing methods that may have a better impact on the environment.

---

1. Sinabell (2001).
2. The EU sponsored "SERIEE" project strives to allocate the environment relevant payments to agriculture, forestry and water management to the various fields of support and indicates for Austria that all support to the sector are directed towards environmental targets, including organic farming. In 1999 ÖPUL was fully integrated into "SERIEE".

standard animal production and accounts for a larger share (roughly 15 per cent) of overall production of sheep, cattle and dairy cows. On average income per family worker on organic farms is about 15 per cent higher than on conventional farms, inducing an expansion of organic farming. Indeed, the supply of organic milk has been promoted to such an extent that it outstrips demand, which has led dairies to sell the excess supply as standard milk products. Normally, excess supply situations are related to prices above market clearing levels, but a particular issue for organic foodstuffs is branding and marketing to enable consumers to distinguish organic products from ordinary food. The information content in existing eco-labels, however, is limited by the multiple eco-labels in use (promoted by associations of organic farmers, direct marketing associations, bio campaigns and individual retail chains with their own eco-labels). As consumers have difficulties in verifying the contents and origins of organic food products, there would appear to be a case for a central standardisation of eco-labels. In addition, the government is actively promoting the production of organic products at the same time as the current excess supply of some organic food products might indicate that the market for expensive high quality organic food has been saturated. The government should thus concentrate on securing framework conditions.

Tourism in Austria has a rather uneven regional distribution with the industry playing a particularly important role in the alpine regions. The environmental problems involved arise from the predominant use of cars to reach tourist areas with associated noise and air pollution, while at the local level environmental problems are mostly related to infrastructure investments in hotels, ski-lifts and slopes and high water consumption for tourism purposes.[168, 169] On the other hand, management of the land also contributes to reducing and limiting the impact of natural disasters, such as avalanches and spring floods. The ÖPUL's emphasis on environmentally friendly agricultural use of land is considered to underpin the maintenance of a suitable alpine landscape. Moreover, farmers are supplying tourist accommodation services (offering almost a third of all private accommodation for tourists, which makes up 18 per cent of the total). Particular concerns have been to maintain pastures in high alpine areas and to prevent depopulation of marginal locations, leading to the present system of income support although these payments only to a small extent are directly linked to the services rendered. In a few cases, payments are made from the tourist industry to the local farms for providing tourist related services. Undoubtedly, preserving small scale farming in the alpine region serves to prevent natural disasters as well as providing a landscape backdrop for tourism. To optimise such possible synergies between agriculture and tourism it should be considered to establish a framework that allows for a more systematic use of compensatory payments (from the tourist industry to farmers) for such positive externalities.

Water management

Austria has relatively little water use per capita (Figure 21). Abstraction – mainly supplied by springs and groundwater sources – is together with pricing of water and water infrastructures the responsibility of the municipals (accounting for 85 per cent of the water supply). Environmental regulation, though, is the responsibility of the central government, which is also providing capital cost subsidies for water related infrastructure.[170] The largest user of water is the industrial sector, accounting for about two-thirds of total abstraction (the highest share of all OECD countries). The household sector's abstraction share is similar to those in other countries, leaving the agriculture sector with a relatively small share of less than 10 per cent of total water utilisation. The latter reflects a modest need for irrigation water, which is typically abstracted directly by the farmers, requiring only a permit that is usually free of charge. Water for livestock is obtained from public water services at the same rates as households.[171]

The structure of *water charges* is determined at the municipal level, allowing a large variation of charge systems among and within the various Länder (for example, Styria has 29 different models).[172] The relatively widespread coverage of water meters (mostly in owner-occupied housing) has allowed volumetric charging systems in a number of municipalities. Other charge models are based on the size of the home, number of toilets or on population equivalents. This has led to a considerable variation in water charges per m^3 from € 0.36 to € 1.82, although the average level is relatively low compared with other OECD countries. The subsidisation of infrastructure investment costs implies that the cost of dimensioning the system may not be fully internalised and water service providers with relatively high fixed costs remain on the market.

Wastewater charges are set by the municipalities and can be based on consumption of fresh water, household sizes, or a lump sum charge. Thus, the variation in the annual costs for an average source is substantial, ranging from € 58 to € 487 per year. Mainly due to high quality standards, wastewater charges are relatively high compared with other European countries.[173] Industrial wastewater must undergo in-plant pre-treatment to be of similar standard as household water, otherwise an additional special charge is introduced to reflect the intensity of pollution in industrial wastewater. Alternatively, if the in-plant pre-treatment is sufficiently effective in cleaning the water according to strict environmental standards, the discharge may be returned to the natural habitat (rivers, lakes, etc.) without charges.[174]

Charges related to water and wastewater are not based on the full cost recovery principle as they only cover somewhat more than half of total costs of water supply and sewage treatment.[175] Investment subsidies from the central government to water infrastructure are fairly widespread, amounting to 20-60 per cent of the

Figure 21.   **Water prices and abstractions**[1]

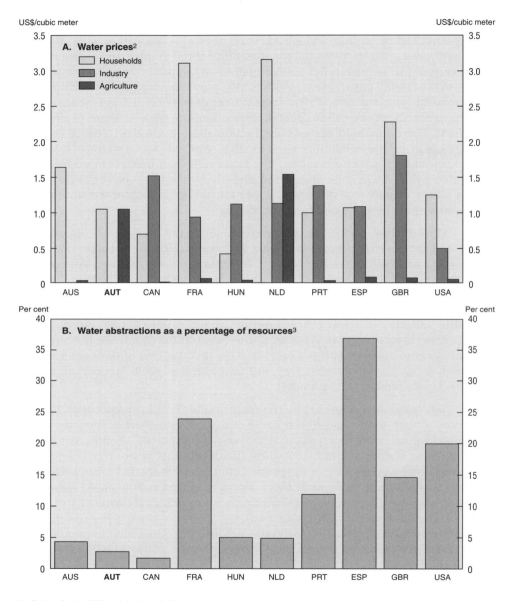

1. Data refer to 1997 or latest available year.
2. Median value for the range of prices for each category.
3. Total abstraction divided by total renewable resources.
Source: Environmental database and OECD (2001), *The Price of Water.*

investment costs over a 25-year period for wastewater treatment plants and about 20 per cent for drinking water investment.[176] The largest part of these subsidies was used for investment in new sewage systems and sewage treatment plants, partly related to an EU requirement of such water-treatment infrastructures to be available for all communities with more than 2 000 inhabitants by 2005.[177] This has certainly improved water quality although at a possibly higher than necessary cost. The widespread subsidisation and service provision confined to administrative districts also imply that relatively small units have to carry a high burden in meeting high standards for infrastructures, indicating possible resource misallocation. Until recently, the situation was further complicated by a lack of incentives for cost-efficiency. However, in the course of the year 2000, the Austrian government has started an initiative towards higher cost-efficiency by amending the National Water Management Act as well as the corresponding guidelines. Keeping in mind the high priority of clean surface and ground water for the Austrian public the Austrian government aims at securing a sufficient level of water-treatment infrastructure investments. This aim could be furthered via a progressive reduction of capital cost subsidies with a parallel rise in the extent of cost recovery built into pricing. Furthermore benchmarking fees could be introduced in order to improve the cost efficiency of water service management. Water-treatment operators should be encouraged to utilise available economies of scale to increase cost efficiency. One step in this direction could be made by stepping up the opportunities to combine water service providers in more efficient water associations.

Waste disposal

Austrian waste policy has been quite effective in terms of reducing waste deposited in landfills and increasing recycling. Between 1989 and 1996 the fraction of household waste destined for recycling increased from 14 per cent to 50 per cent, and the proportion of waste finally deposited in landfill – after reprocessing or incineration – decreased from three-quarters to 43 per cent.[178] This development can be ascribed to a combination of regulations, economic instruments and "voluntary agreements". Regulations in place for the treatment of household waste concern the packaging and collection of biodegradable waste, among others, while the most important industry regulation is the obligation to take back and treat packaging waste. Waste collection fees are either based on flat rates (per person or per household) or variable rates (related to weight or volume of collected units), and, particularly in the former case, are only to a minor degree designed to create incentives for minimising waste.[179] Moreover, waste collection fees are not particularly based on the full cost recovery principle as total revenues may exceed costs.[180] In addition, a substantial amount of waste separation at the household level is taking place on a voluntary basis.

However, recycling quotas must be set in sensible ways to ensure environmentally friendly and efficient waste management, as illustrated by a cost benefit analysis of recycling plastics from household waste, commissioned by the Ministry of Environment.[181] It concludes that the costs of the present system exceed its benefits by a fair margin every year. Moreover, important interdependencies with other environmental policies may not always be recognised, such as with fuel taxation. If the production of a given good has a higher transport intensity than involved in recycling the same good, then low fuel taxation would conflict with the recycling objective.[182] Alternative systems to recycling quotas may be preferred, such as differentiated fees targeted directly at the associated externalities.[183] Indeed, the Austrian experience with increasing landfill charges points in this direction. They are set according to the hazard potential of the waste and on the equipment of the landfill sites, underpinning the development where waste treatment is increasingly moving away from landfills and with the remaining landfill waste increasingly being shifted towards more technologically advanced landfills.

In the case of contaminated disused industrial sites, the legal framework stipulates that the responsible company has the financial duty – with no time limit – to clean them up. If the responsible company cannot be obliged to do so, the responsibility may fall on the property owner and only otherwise it becomes a federal responsibility.[184] So far only 57 out of 158 registered contaminated sites have undergone complete clean up and another 53 are in the process of being cleaned. Public funding covered nearly 80 per cent of total remediation costs in 1997 before declining to just above 50 per cent in 1999.

Conclusions and assessment

Environmental concerns are deeply embedded in the political debate in Austria and materialise in various aspects of policy setting, including in the formulation of regulations to protect the environment, in the planning of major infrastructure projects, and in the setting of ambitious environmental goals and international commitments. An evaluation of Austrian policies needs to take into account the high environmental standards found in Austria and substantial financial and economic resources are devoted to meet Austria's environmental objectives. However, the lack of a systematic evaluation of policies' environmental impact and thus of an integration of environmental concerns and policy formulation means that targets are set at ambitious levels without consideration of the implied costs and with little possibility for ex-post evaluations. Furthermore, policies directed at similar objectives are not well co-ordinated, as witnessed by the CO_2 emission reduction strategy and the implicit high and varying cost associated with the expected CO_2 emission reductions in different policies. Introducing a consistent use of cost-benefit analysis across policies would provide the basis for an integrated policy planning process.[185] Policies could thereby attach similar values to reducing CO_2 and thus serve to reduce overall abatement costs and enhance policy effectiveness and co-ordination across the Austrian federation. In addition, cost-benefit analyses could be used as an efficient feedback and evaluation instrument.

Policies to pursue environmental objectives with respect to CO_2 emissions have until now been mostly based on subsidies as well as command-and-control instruments. However, to reach Austria's ambitious environmental objectives in a cost-efficient manner a greater reliance on economic instruments is warranted, like integrating the current system of taxes on energy and fuels with a properly modified CO_2 tax, which would increase incentives for using less CO_2 intensive energy sources. Such a change should be accompanied by the abolition of the various tax exemptions in place at present that are not environmentally motivated so as to ensure similar abatement costs across the economy. In addition, such a measure would remove the current tax advantage of diesel as well as making renewable energy sources more competitive. In the Austrian context, however, a CO_2 tax would generate a rent for large competitive hydropower plants, which cannot be competed away through an expansion of electricity generated by hydropower – given the restrictions on developing new hydropower plants. Such a CO_2 tax generated rent would then have to be removed through additional taxation. Insofar as it is difficult to implement a CO_2 tax for competitive reasons, alternative schemes mitigating the competitive disadvantage of a CO_2 tax without diminishing environmental incentives could be the introduction of tax credits or the expansion of the green certificate system, emission permit schemes, including cap-and-trade systems with permits being grand–fathered according to past electricity production and based on average industry emissions.[186] Indeed, emission trading would allow participants in the scheme to receive monetary compensation for implementing new and environmentally friendly technologies as the associated reduction in CO_2 emissions can be sold, ensuring that the most intensive emitters would face the strongest incentives and thus ensuring a cost-efficient lowering of CO_2 emissions.[187]

Until now, the support system for promoting renewable energies has relied on providing investment subsidies. The higher reliance on market based instruments in the new support system within a liberalised electricity market is most welcome. The deregulation of Austrian energy markets is also beneficial from an environmental point of view, as competitive price structures combined with taxation of polluting emissions, such as CO_2, NO_x and SO_x, would serve to equalise abatement costs across different types of primary energy sources.

The promotion of renewable energy sources within a liberalised electricity market without a tax on CO_2 emissions is a non-trivial problem as the technologies have not evolved to a degree where the cost of electricity generated by renewable energy source can compete directly with marginal conventional power plants (with the exception of large-scale hydro power plants). The targets for how large a share of electricity generation originating from renewable energy are somewhat arbitrary and are formulated within the context of specific environmental problems. The cost-ineffectiveness of the guaranteed feed-in-tariffs is revealed by the high and varied implicit values of CO_2 for the various policies across Austria. One of the main advantages of moving from a subsidy based support system for promoting renewable energies to a market based one is that the latter allows for the equalisation of abatement costs across projects, which assures the achievement of an environmental target with the lowest possible economic burden. The variation in guaranteed feed-in-tariffs is biasing the incentive structure in complex ways. Thus, a uniform structure for feed-in-tariffs across Austria should replace the present system with Länder-determined feed-in-tariffs. On the other hand, the possibility of "green certificate" trading allows for a welcome element of flexibility, for example in avoiding unnecessary transmission costs. However, the restriction of "green certificate" trading to only concern electricity generated by small-scale hydropower plants appears overly restrictive, as it is preventing the cost of expanding renewable energy sources from being minimised. An additional consideration should be the dynamic adjustment of minimum feed-in tariffs in line with technological progress in the non-hydro electricity generation to ensure support rates that remain constant in real terms to avoid an excessive expansion of particular types of renewable energy sources.

The use of command-and-control instruments has limited the environmental impact of transport – particularly transit traffic – but has failed to limit the increase of alpine transit traffic itself. Moreover, the success of moving freight to the railway system by providing infrastructures for promoting co-transportation hinges on other countries engaging in similar investments, postponing the date when such transport solutions can be implemented on a large scale. Thus, the regulation of transit traffic should rely on bringing into line the marginal cost of transit with the associated external costs. This could be obtained through a road pricing system that takes into account the environmental costs of lorries driving through sensitive alpine regions, requiring an adaptation of the pertinent EU legislation. This would improve incentives for hauliers to use only the most modern and effective vehicles in this particular area.

Reducing CO_2 emissions through urban renewal projects is a very expensive policy, which might not be justified by other associated benefits. In addition, subsidies to improve the thermal efficiency in housing benefit the owners twice: through a lower energy bill (possibly shared by owner and tenant) and a quality improvement of the property, leading to higher property prices. The latter effect would indicate that a relaxation of rent control regulations would enable landlords to recuperate the investment costs of improving the thermal efficiency. The complementary policy of expanding district heating and combined heat and power plants (CHPs) through large-scale subsidies may have pushed the coverage beyond its efficient limit. In addition, the ongoing liberalisation of the electricity markets implies that the CHPs will be delivering services to a competitive electricity market and a non-competitive heating market. That kind of structures might lead to cross-subsidisation from the non-competitive to the competitive segment. Such competition problems should be solved before further expanding the coverage of CHPs.

Within the public debate there is a perception that public transport is friendlier to the environment than private cars, leading to a policy objective of better balancing the use of private cars with public transportation. Policies to minimise the environmental impact of passenger transport should focus on bringing the marginal cost of using cars into line with their environmental externalities through appropriate taxation as well as minimising the environmental impact per passenger in public transportation.

The considerable reliance on subsidies to promote various environmental objectives should be reconsidered. The relatively high costs of water-treatment provision reflects high standards as well as individual units being rather small and not facing pressures to control costs. A phasing out of capital cost subsidies would allow a move towards full recovery pricing principles, thus revealing particularly inefficient water-treatment providers and improving resource allocation. Pressures to lower costs could include the introduction of a standardised charge structure. In addition, insofar as high costs are the result of inefficiency in size, the formation of cost-reducing associations of water-treatment providers should be exploited further. The setting of waste collection and treatment charges should be determined by the full cost recovery principle – including environmental costs – to avoid cross-subsidisation leading to misallocation of resources. In addition, quotas might lead to an inefficient approach to waste collection and treatment as their use risks restraining the implementation of new technologies.

Unlike in many other countries, the agricultural sector in Austria is not the origin of general environmental problems. However, resource allocation might be improved if the support system were changed from production-method-oriented to be targeted at specific environmental outcomes. Valuation of the latter can be achieved by cost-benefit analysis. The newly experienced excess supply of some organically-farmed products may be the reflection of a need for a common and unified system of eco-labels, but could also reflect a saturation of the market for high price and high quality organic products. Both arguments highlight that more room should be provided for market determined outcomes while administrative measures should focus on framework conditions. The perceived positive effects of agricultural environmentally friendly use of land on tourism should be evaluated through the introduction of cost-benefit analysis which could form the basis for a framework that allows for a systematic use of compensatory payments for such positive externalities, leading to an optimisation of such synergies. Combined with a redirection of subsidies to be linked directly to the provision of tourism related services and landscape preservation this would improve the targeting of subsidies by directing resources to the areas with the largest scope for tourism. In addition, although there are no general problems of nutrient leakages, local environmental problems arising from agriculture requires local solutions, such as the establishment of farm level nutrient accounts combined with taxation of nutrient surpluses, rather than be solved with broadly based programmes.

Notes

1. Simulation results on the Secretariat's Interlink model (focusing on traditional international transmission mechanisms) indicate that about 50 per cent of the effects on Austrian growth of an upswing in the United States will materialise after six months and the full effect only with a lag of 18-24 months. However, due to the relatively little direct trade between Austria and the United States, the effects on Austrian growth of an upswing in the United States are only two-thirds of the effects on Euro area growth.

2. Focusing only on manufactured goods, the export market growth since 1995 has amounted to more than 9½ per cent as compared with just above 6¼ per cent the preceding decade.

3. Czerny *et al.* (2001).

4. The Austrian National Accounts statistics do not publish employment data on full-time equivalents. The latter can only be deduced from the annual labour force surveys and can thus not be used to follow within-year developments.

5. Pork consumption is about three times higher than beef consumption, implying a relatively larger weight for pork meat in the consumer price index.

6. See OECD (1999*a*).

7. In national accounting the proceeds from selling the mobile phone licenses are booked as negative expenditures.

8. See Breuss (2001).

9. See OECD (1998*a* and 1999*a*).

10. See Van den Noord, Paul and Christopher Heady (2001. See also: Leibfritz *et al.* (1997)).

11. See Joumard (2001).

12. The assumptions of this projection are: an increase of fertility to a total fertility rate of 1.50, an increase of life expectancy to 82.0 years for males and 87.0 years for females by the year 2050, a long-term immigration of 80 000 people per year leading to a net immigration of 20 000 people per year. The total population is projected to increase over the next 30 years to 8.386 million people (+3.4 per cent); but beginning in 2032 the population is expected to decrease as a result of an excess of deaths over births.

13. For an international comparison of projected old-age dependency ratios and pension-related spending see OECD (2001*a*). See also Guger and Mayrhuber (2001).

14. Estimates of the implicit taxation of continued work suggest that the Austrian pension system provides significant incentives for early retirement, even after a series of reforms over the past few years. See Hofer and Koman (2001).

15. The main assumptions are: unemployment is assumed to fall from 5.9 per cent in 2000 to some 4 per cent in 2050; labour productivity increases by 1.9 per cent annually,

which translates into annual real GDP growth of 1.7 per cent, given a declining labour force; the labour force participation rate increases by some 18 per cent over the next five decades, with an increase of some 33½ and 44 percentage points for males and females, respectively, in the age group of 55 to 64.

16. See OECD (1998a).

17. See OECD (1998a). In the 1997 pension reform, the base for pension entitlement of early retirees has been extended to the 18 best years of a persons work history, but this is only being phased in from 2003 onwards.

18. The replacement ratio has been found generous in Austria, see Hofer and Komann (2001).

19. No income taxes, capital gains taxes and speculation taxes have to be paid for private retirement provisions. Furthermore, an interest-dependent bonus is given (3.5 per cent in 2000 and 4.5 per cent in 2001). With the tax reform of October 2000, a general tax allowance was abolished and instead a new additional bonus for private retirement provisions of 5.5 per cent introduced. Therefore, in 2001 the total bonus amounts to 10 per cent, up to a ceiling of € 1 000 investment per year. When the system was created in 1999 the original idea was that in case of emergency the funds invested by private households could be taken out of the pension fund provided the bonuses and the saved taxes are paid back to the government. This flexibility was withdrawn soon after the introduction, as it was felt that it would privilege pension investment funds over other pension-related instruments (Pensionskassen), and this might partly explain why the number of pension investment funds sold is far below expectations.

20. In early 2001 the highway user fees (Autobahnvignette) had to be increased in order to prevent the market based revenues of the ASFINAG to decline below the 50 per cent hurdle.

21. OECD (1998a and 1999a).

22. The ultimate financial responsibility of governments is apparent from the fact that privatisations of public sector corporations in Austria as well as in other OECD countries are often associated with debt take-overs by the government. If such take-overs do not take place, the selling price of public sector corporations is reduced accordingly.

23. See Fiedler (2001).

24. FGG (2000).

25. Kropf et al. (2001).

26. See Aufgabenreformkommission (2001).

27. See in particular OECD (1996 and 1997).

28. For an account of the new revenue sharing arrangement see Lehner (2001).

29. For Germany, such effects have been found by Baretti and Lichtblau (2000), and by Berthold et al. (2001). See also Zhuravskaya (2001).

30. See OECD (1999a).

31. See Pollan (2001).

32. Moreover, general training by employees is partly financed by the labour office.

33. See Walther (1999).

34. See Mayrhuber (2000).

35. In 1997 23½ per cent of all occupations in Austria were shorter than one year. See Mayrhuber (2000).

36. According to the 2000 micro-census. Part-time employment denotes employment with less than 36 hours worked per week.

37. See Evans *et al.* (2001). See also OECD (2001*b*).

38. Statistics on work commissioned by firms from self-employed (*freie Dienstverträge*) are only available from June 1998 onwards, which precludes comparisons with their expansion prior to the increase in social security charges. Total social security charges for both small-hours jobs and work commissioned by firms from self-employed are still lower than for regular employment.

39. Other leaves with specific training programmes do not require new hirings, such as leaves for older people for whom preferential support rates apply.

40. It has been argued that conditioning unemployment benefits on the wage level in the last job might imply a disincentive for the unemployed to accept a lower-paid job. However, to the extent the old regulation has help up reservation wages this is not true.

41. See Winter-Ebmer (1998).

42. See OECD (2000*b*) and OECD (2001*c*).

43. The re-employment guarantee for formerly employed recipients was left unchanged at two years.

44. Biffl (2000).

45. See OECD (1994) and OECD (2001*c*).

46. See Biffl (2000).

47. See Riggs (2001); OECD (2001*d*) and OECD (2001*e*).

48. See Österreichisches Institut für Wirtschaftsforschung and Institut für höhere Studien (2000).

49. Evaluation studies for active labour market measures in Austria include: Biffl *et al.* (1996). Lechner *et al.* (2000). Fehr-Duda *et al.* (1996). Bundesministerium für Arbeit, Gesundheit und Soziales (1999). Lechner *et al.* (2000). Lassnig *et al.* (1999). Blumberger (2000). Huber and Walterskirchen (1999). Lassnigg and Steiner (2000). Österreichisches Institut für Wirtschaftsforschung, Institut für höhere Studien (2000).

50. See Fay (1996). Martin (1998). Mitterauer *et al.* (1999. Hagen and Steiner (2000). OECD (2001*c*).

51. See OECD (1999*b* and 2001*f*). Also, Hagen and Steiner (2000).

52. The share of hirings without financial support appears lower if the responses of the employees are also taken into consideration. See Mitterauer *et al.* (1999).

53. See Black *et al.* (2001).

54. Integration of local employers into territorial employment pacts appears to proceed sluggish, however. See Österreichisches Institut für Wirtschaftsforschung, Institut für höhere Studien (2000).

55. In 2000, 10.2 of the dependent employees were foreigners. Some 10 per cent of the foreign dependent employees are EU nationals. See Biffl (2001).

56. Walterskirchen and Biffl (2001).

57. At the age of 14 or 15 young people have the following options of upper secondary education: secondary high schools (at present absorbing some 20 per cent of an age cohort); secondary vocational schools designed to provide both a basic understanding

of a particular field to skilled worker level and broader general education (some 15 per cent of an age cohort); secondary technical and vocational colleges designed to provide advanced general and vocational training to higher-skilled worker level (some 25 per cent of an age cohort); the dual apprenticeship system providing within-company training along with instructions at a vocational school.

58. The federal University Studies Act of 1997 entitled universities to develop new curricula in their own responsibility.

59. See OECD (2001*g*).

60. The fee is € 363 per semester (Sch 5 000). The government estimates that the proceeds – to be used for investment in the university system – will total more than € 145 million per year.

61. In the United Kingdom the narrowing down of the multi-layered structure of the institutional set-up for competition policies is considered important to promote effective regulation. See OECD (2001*h*).

62. The example of the United States shows that a multiplicity of enforcement institutions and enforcement methods poses a continual challenge for maintaining co-ordination and consistency. Despite no history of conflicts among the institutions the system is nevertheless considered costly. See OECD (1999*c*).

63. The size of such fines should be sufficiently large to ensure compliance in order to avoid firms – particularly large ones – to consider such fines as merely administrative costs. Several countries – Canada, Ireland, Japan and the United States and with the United Kingdom considering – have provisions of using prison terms to ensure compliance. Until now only the United States has used such provisions actively. Furthermore, such fines in the United States are normally on a per day of non-compliance basis, leading to cases with accumulated fines of several million dollars.

64. The electricity and telecommunication sectors have independent sector regulators, the Elektrizitäts-Control GmbH and the Telecom Control GmbH. Their findings are referred to sector specific commissions (Elektrizitäts-Control Commission and Telekom-Control Commission), which then can issue administrative fines if companies are found not to comply with the issued regulation. The decisions of the Elektrizitäts Control Commission can be referred to the Cartel Court, while those of the Telekom Control Commission can be referred to the Administrative Court (*Verwaltungsgerichtshof*) or the Constitutional Court (*Verfassungsgerichtshof*). The split between regulator and commission has been introduced as the Austrian constitution allows administrative bodies to issue fines only to a limited extent.

65. See OECD (2001*i*).

66. Regulatory capture refers to a situation where regulators – often inadvertently – advocate the interest of the producers they are intended to regulate. With or without the use of sector-specific regulators, risks of regulatory capture can be reduced by increasing the transparency and accountability of regulatory decision making.

67. For a discussion of appropriate roles for sector-specific regulators and general competition authorities, see OECD (1999*d*); and OECD (2001*f*).

68. For details, see Ministry of Economic Affairs and Labour (2001).

69. For a detailed discussion of the issues involved, see Steiner (2001).

70. While the consumer has the free choice of a supplier and is priced accordingly, "actual" consumption of electricity occurs from the pool of all suppliers delivering electricity into the net.

71. The national high voltage transmission grid (Verbund) is owned by a regulated monopoly with transmission charges set by the regulator.

72. Moreover, charges vary across the Länder and with different levels of grid loss costs, all factors combined adding to a diffuse picture.

73. Present rules for unbundling follow EU guidelines. See EU Commission (2001).

74. On 26 April 2001, the OECD Council adopted a recommendation encouraging Members to consider and balance the benefits and costs of structural versus behavioural measures in addressing problems likely to arise in situations in which a regulated firm is or may in future be operating simultaneously in a non-competitive activity and a potentially competitive complementary activity.

75. Steiner (2001) op. cit.

76. For examples, see OECD (2001j).

77. Bundesministerium für Wirtschaft und Arbeit (2000).

78. A part of the Austrian telecommunication regulator – the Telekom-Control GmbH – formally ceased to exist on 31 March 2001 when it became part of the Austrian Regulatory Authority for Broadcasting and Telecommunications, which assumed, among other functions, Telekom-Control GmbH's function as an agent to the Telekom-Control Commission. The RTR is also responsible for broadcasting regulation.

79. EU Commission (2000a).

80. By mid-2000 there were more than 200 interconnection agreements and nearly 50 instances where the regulator determined interconnection charges.

81. ECB (2001).

82. The UMTS auction in November 2000 yielded € 828.5 million and allocated six licenses to six bidders in the paired segment, which should provide for increased competition in the mobile phone market, once the system has been developed.

83. OECD (2001k).

84. Such calls refer to a direct call from a fixed-line or mobile telephone to a mobile phone where it terminates.

85. For further discussion of the high fixed-to-mobile tariffs and roaming charges issues, see OECD (2001l).

86. See EU Commission (2000b).

87. OECD (2001m).

88. Five providers have been accredited for the use of electronic signatures and the monitoring body is the Telekom Control Commission.

89. Transport services and the network have been separately incorporated in Denmark, France, the Netherlands, Sweden and the United Kingdom. OECD (2001j).

90. See OECD (2001f).

91. The EC has proposed to lower the limit to 50 grams by 2007, see EU Commission (2000c).

92. OECD (1999e).

93. For a discussion of competition issues in the postal sector, including problems related to universal service obligations, see OECD (1999f).

94. Commission Recommendation for the 2001 Broad Guidelines of the Economic Policies of the Member States and the Community.

95. The text of public invitations to tender can be retrieved from the Internet pages of the newspaper "Wiener Zeitung".

96. See Boyland and Nicoletti (2001).

97. Not all *Länder* continue to provide such public deficiency – *de facto* insolvency – guarantees.

98. The credit rating of Bank Austria (at the time partly owned by the City of Vienna) will be lowered from Aa2 to Aa3 in connection with the finalisation of its sale to the German HypoVereinsbank.

99. From mid-2002 onwards, previously unidentified owners of saving accounts exceeding € 14 535 can access their accounts only after their identity has been reported to the Financial Intelligence Unit (FIU) and the latter does not object.

100. The following international correction of telecommunication shares also affected Telekom Austria shares, which fell by about a third in the first months after the privatisation, although the share has strengthened since.

101. Ministry of Economic Affairs and Labour (2001).

102. The act also creates a legal basis for the participation of the Austrian Securities Authority in international co-operation in the area of supervision and allows for the authorisation of new supervised markets based on alternative trading platforms.

103. B*ürges* also issues undated tradable bearer securities with a minimum redemption period of 10 years to raise long-term capital for SMEs, although this instrument still has to attract market interest. Nevertheless, possible hurting household investor confidence in purchasing shares from new privatisation.

104. The Austrian property tax, measured as a share of GDP is the second lowest in the EU. See Joumard (2001).

105. In order to make the financial supervisor fully independent a qualified two-thirds parliamentary majority would have been necessary, but could not be reached.

106. The large involvement of Ministry of Finance in financial supervision is unusual compared with the practice of most other OECD member countries.

107. The Financial Market Supervisory Authority will have a managing board of two persons, a supervisory board of six persons and an advisory board of eight persons. Half of the members of the managing and the supervisory boards are nominated by the OeNB and the other half by the Ministry of Finance.

108. The institutions will be charged fees and the federal government will make a fixed annual contribution of € 3½ million.

109. In Germany, the government has tabled a draft law for the creation of a single supervisory body.

110. The FMSA may commission the OeNB to carry out on-site inspections in the fields of credit and market risks in OeNB's name and responsibility.

111. OECD (2001*j*).

112. This chapter forms part of the Secretariat's three-year programme on sustainable development. For a summary of this programme, see O'Brien and Vourc'h (2001).

113. See OECD (1995).

114. In July 2001, an agreement was reached in Bonn by all participating countries, with the exception of the United States, on a broad framework for implementing the Kyoto Protocol. Decisions are still outstanding on important matters, such as compliance mecha-

nisms and sinks, making it difficult to assess the likelihood of timely ratification, or the specific implications of the Protocol with respect to any one Party.

115. Recently, there has been some concentration of federal competencies with the present government's creation of the Ministry of Agriculture, Forestry, Environment and Water Management. However, other ministries have retained their enforcement powers in relevant environmentally-related areas like environmental taxes (as part of the Ministry of Finance's overall responsibility for tax policies) and industrial regulation (Ministry of Economic Affairs and Labour).

116. Federal Ministry of Agriculture, Forestry, Environment and Water (2000).

117. For a description of various valuation techniques, see O'Brien and Vourc'h (2001).

118. OECD (2000*b*).

119. See table 2 in O'Brien and Vourc'h (2001) for an overview of legal practises in various OECD countries.

120. Firms' compliance costs are equal to the investment costs of reaching the publicly-determined standards and additional costs for below legal standards pollution or emissions only insofar as economic instruments, such as environmental taxes, are in place.

121. The first numerical target for reducing CO_2 emissions was introduced after the 1988 Toronto Conference when Austria adopted a national target of reducing CO_2 emissions by 20 per cent in 2005 as compared with the 1988 level

122. OECD (1999*g*).

123. In general economic instruments aims at ensuring that the value of the marginal damage to the environment is equal to the marginal cost of abatement, thereby securing that polluters pay in accordance to the damage they inflict on the environment and that the cost of reaching a given level of abatement is minimised. The advantage of introducing international trading is that these advantages of economic instruments are being extended to the international level.

124. However, taking into account temperature and production variations, Austria's CO_2 emission in 1992 and 1993 was 7½ per cent lower than if production and temperature patterns had been normal. Overall for the period 1990 to 1997, the measured CO_2 emission was 2.5 per cent lower than when adjusted for variations in temperature and production. See Schleicher *et al.* (1999).

125. IEA (1998).

126. The exemptions are, in the case of the energy tax: coal altogether, gas used for other purposes than heating as well as gas and electricity used for the production and transport of energy and in the case of the mineral oil tax: fuels used for aeroplanes, ships and trains, refineries, blast furnaces, combined heat and power plants and electricity generation.

127. OECD database on environmentally related taxes.

128. The revenue of an environmentally related tax is a poor gauge for its effectiveness, as the most effective environmental taxes will have close to zero revenue.

129. However, other elements of the tax system have negative effects on the environment as they promote transport activities, as in the case of deductibility of commuting cost. Indeed, there is a risk that road transport is promoted over of public transport as the value of the deductions for commuting by car is around twice as high as for commuting

by public transportation subject to availability rules, although the final assessment would have to include all subsidies to the different types of transport. Kletzan (2000).

130. Moreover, other exemptions from the road transport duty include, among others, army vehicles, lorries for the transport of household waste, circus lorries, agriculture vehicles in agricultural use, taxis and rental cars.

131. In the mid-1990s, taxation of private road transports was somewhat higher than associated infrastructure investment costs. Moreover, additional external costs arising from road transport, including traffic accidents and less easily measured costs as noise pollution, environmental damages and traffic congestion, has been estimated to be nearly € 3.6 billion. Prior to EU accession, taxes and charges related to road transport amounted to more than 90 per cent of such costs. Consequently, such taxes and charges only covered about half of the total associated costs, adding external costs and infrastructure costs together. Bundesministerium für Wissenschaft und Verkehr (1997).

132. The structural loss situation of ASFINAG makes explicit guarantees and full ownership by the Austrian Republic necessary. See ASFINAG (2001).

133. Friedl and Steininger (2001) conclude that explicit costs increases in the form of road pricing is more efficient to achieve environmentally sustainable transport than implicit measures like congestion and regulation.

134. The ongoing implementation of the Green tax reform in Germany implies that fuel taxes are being increased, increasing the scope for higher Austrian fuel taxes (see OECD 2001f).

135. Economy-wide effects of a 10 per cent increase in the differential in transport fuel prices between Germany and Austria is estimated to lower sales of gasoline and diesel by around 3.0 and 3.4 per cent, respectively. See Puwein (1996).

136. Pre-tax prices on unleaded gasoline and automotive diesel are generally higher than in other European OECD countries, which could be an indication of limited competition in the markets for fuels. Environmentally motivated taxes may thus serve to magnify differences in product market competition, thus exaggerate existing differences in abatement costs across fuel types.

137. Another (non necessarily cost-efficient) solution is the implementation of new technologies as in the case of Vienna's bus fleet, which consists of nearly 80 per cent LPG (Liquid Petroleum Gas) driven buses, of which 94 per cent are equipped with three-ways catalytic converters. (Central European Initiative (1999) Towards Sustainable Transport in the CEI Countries, Vienna.). More generally, the high share of LPG-buses may be explained by the tax-exemption from the mineral oil tax when used for public transportation.

138. See OECD (2001n) and O'Brien et al. (2001), op. cit. for a more detailed discussion.

139. Other forms of international transport, such as air and sea transport, pay no fuel tax – in accordance with international treaties – implying incentives that are poorly aligned with externalities.

140. O'Brien and Vourc'h (2001).

141. Koeppl et al. (1996).

142. In many proposals for energy taxes a recycling of tax revenues is suggested to migrate the negative effects. The two most prominent candidates in the debate are either a lowering of labour taxes, which typically benefits labour intensive domestically orientated service sectors, or compensation of (capital-intensive) export orientated sectors. See for example Breuss and Steininger (1998).

143. As a result, the real gross investment in road structures has fallen by 40 per cent over the decade leading to 1997 compared with a 20 per cent increase in railway structures. This, however, has failed to make an impact on passenger transport's road market share of 90 per cent, while for goods the road market share has increased from just above half to nearly two-thirds. Puwein (1999).

144. While not being the main cause, low fuel prices are certainly not contributing to a reduction of transit traffic. It should also be mentioned that Austria has a positive balance of international transport services.

145. The Federal Ministry of Transport, Innovation and Technology funds a number of research projects in cleaner mobility technologies as an additional measure to diminish the negative environmental impact from transport.

146. Calculations, using the so-called "willingness-to-pay" method, suggest that the internal rate of return of establishing a national park east of Vienna ("Donau-Auen" national park) was similar or higher than constructing a hydroelectric power plant in the same place. See Kosz (1996) pp. 109-127.

147. The similar rate of subsidies across renewable energy projects, however, may have very different effects on production costs, depending on depreciation rates and shares of capital cost of total costs.

148. In addition the federal government is providing subsidies for the construction of power plants using non-hydro renewable energy sources, amounting to € 16.9 million in 2000. In addition some Länder (Vienna) also provides investment subsidies, reaching up 30 or 50 per cent of construction depending on type of renewable energy.

149. The purchasing obligation, the feed-in-tariffs and the extra grid-charge together form the so-called "3-pillar-system" for promoting electricity generated by renewable energy sources.

150. The green certificates are issued by the supplier along with the sales of the electricity and form the basis for verification. Trading of green certificates are also being introduced in other countries like Denmark and Australia. See OECD (2000c) and OECD (2001e).

151. Combined heat and power plants together with district heating projects have been promoted by grants amounting to € 109 million since 1984, implying an average investment subsidy of 10 per cent. In one Land (Steiermark) the subsidy rate for district heating projects based on biomass was until 2000 up to 50 per cent when it was lowered to between 30 and 40 per cent. The subsidy for ordinary district heating projects could, prior to 1993, reach 30 per cent.

152. See OECD (1999h).

153. Calculated as the implied subsidy (the difference between the average guaranteed feed-in price and the average production cost of conventionally generated electricity) multiplied by the amount of electricity replaced, which would amount to nearly 140 GWh from natural gas power plants and 62 GWh from coal powered plants.

154. Amounting to one of the highest shares for railways in OECD-Europe. OECD (1998b).

155. Nevertheless, the expansion of public transportation in Vienna is expected to reduce CO_2 emissions by nearly 300 000 tonnes by 2010.

156. Estimations point to a quadrupling or more of goods related road traffic with the prospective EU-member countries in eastern Europe within 10 years after their eventual accession to the EU, while the similar increase for railway transport would amount to a doubling. See Puwein (2001).

157. Since 1980 minimum standards for thermal insulation in new buildings have progressively become more stringent. Mandatory efficiency standards are in place for thermal insulation of buildings; efficiency of space heating and hot water equipment; individual metering of heat together with efficiency labels for household appliances.

158. The individual subsidy may range from € 29 to €58 per m², but is limited to one-third of the overall project costs. The tenant or the dwelling owner must finance the remaining project costs.

159. Effectively these estimates are biased downwards as the discount factor for future CO_2 reductions have implicitly been set at zero.

160. In terms of energy use, however, the plants still rely on relatively CO_2 intensive fuels with nearly half of the plants using oil as compared with almost a third using natural gas, while the remaining plants are powered by biomass or waste incineration

161. The efficiency of district heating is a function of housing density and number of power stations feeding the network as on average 28 per cent of the heat energy is lost during transportation of the water in the pipelines. Bundesministerium fur Umwelt, Jugend und Familie (1998).

162. Under the District Heating Promotion Act, about € 52 million were disbursed between 1984 and 1995. The Act terminated in 1993 but funding continued thereafter.

163. IEA (1998).

164. The number of farms receiving support is around 150 000 with an average size of some 14 hectare. The average subsidy is about € 3 600 per farm under the ÖPUL and € 5 800 per farm in total subsidies.

165. ÖPUL is the abbreviation for "Österreichisches Programm zur Förderung einer umweltgerechten, extensiven und den natürlichen Lebensraum schützenden Landwirtschaft".

166. In addition, national law regulates – through norms and standards – water protection, nature conservation, and the use of pesticides and fertilisers. The latter was taxed in the period 1986-95 with a consequent 10 per cent decrease in demand, but was abolished upon EU accession.

167. For an exposé of the interaction between organic farming and sustainable development, see for example Stagl (2001).

168. Among other initiatives to minimise the negative environmental impact of local transport and to promote environmentally friendly tourism, it can be mentioned that pilot studies of car-free tourism in the ski resorts Bad Hofgastein and Werfenweng are being undertaken to develop models for minimising the negative environmental impact of local car transport.

169. About 10 per cent of all slopes have required alteration to the natural drop of the slopes.

170. The Water Law allows for the formation of local water associations (Wassergenossenschaften, WG and Wasserverbande, WV), when these prove more effective in reaching objectives regarding water. Around one-half of all municipalities is a member of such an association. Rudolph (1998).

171. OECD (1999i).

172. In some regions water suppliers provide financial indemnification for reduced use of fertiliser and pesticides.

173. Rudolph (1998).

174. OECD (1999i).

175. Full cost recovery prices to all users should in principle include capital costs, costs of environmental damages and scarcity rent components. The EU Framework Water Directive sets objectives for water protection at the same time as it states explicitly that cross-subsidisation should be avoided, although the directive contains provisions for guaranteeing access to basic volumes for household water at "social" charge rates. Normally marginal cost pricing would be an optimal pricing strategy, but with increasing rate of return such a strategy would lead to continuously under-funded water works.

176. Water-related subsidies are reaching 30 per cent for industries and up to 60 per cent for municipalities.

177. In 1999 about 90 per cent of financial support from the Environmental and Water Management Fund was allocated to investment in wastewater disposal. See Kommunal Kredit (1999).

178. Federal Ministry of Environment, Youth and Family Affairs (1998).

179. A 1999 survey revealed that only 8 per cent of the Vienna population were aware of the costs of waste collection.

180. The Fiscal Compensation Law ("Finanzausgleichsgesetz") stipulates that the annual revenue may not exceed 200 per cent of the annual costs.

181. Federal Ministry of Environment, Youth and Family Affairs (1998).

182. ECMT (2000).

183. See Pearce (1998).

184. Since 1989, about € 218 million has been earmarked for cleaning up contaminated industrial sites.

185. See OECD (2001o), Chapter VI on the experiences of OECD countries of cost-benefit analysis using to encourage environmentally sustainable growth.

186. See OECD (1999j) for a survey and discussion of existing programmes as well as OECD (2001p).

187. See Kletzan and Köppl (2001) for a detailed discussion of the issues involved.

Bibliography

ASFINAG (2001),
   Lagebericht über das Geschäftsjahr 2000, Wien.

Aufgabenreformkommission (2001),
   Bericht der Aufgabenreformkommission, mimeo, Wien.

Baretti, Christian and Karl Lichtblau (2000),
   A tax on tax revenues, CES*ifo Working paper* No. 333.

Berthold, Norbert, Stefan Drews and Eric Thode (2001),
   "Die föderale Ordnung in Deutschland – Motor oder Bremse des wirstschaftlichen Wachstums?", *Zeitschrift für Wirtschaftspolitik* No. 2.

Biffl, Gudrun (2000),
   "Deregulation of placement services – The case of Austria", *Austrian Economic Quarterly* No. 1/2000, WIFO.

Biffl, Gudrun (2001),
   Arbeitsmarktrelevante Effekte der Ausländerintegration in Österreich – Studie des Österreichischen Instituts für Wirtschaftsforschung im Auftrag des Bundesministers für Wirtschaft und Arbeit, mimeo, Wien.

Biffl, Gudrun, Helmut Hofer and Karl Pichelmann (1996),
   Sozialökonomische Beschäftigungsprojekte und soziale Kursmassnahmen, in AMS, Ergebnisse der inovativen Arbeitsmarktpolitik, Wien.

Black, D. A., M. C. Berger, J. N. Noel and J. A. Smith (2001),
   "Is the threat of training more effective than training itself? Experimental evidence from ui claimants profiling" in Lechner, M. and F. Pfeiffer (eds), *Econometric evaluation*, Heidelberg.

Blumberger, Walter (2000),
   Wege aus der Arbeitslosigkeit – Evaluierung des Unternehmensgründungsprogrammes des Arbeitsmarktservice Österreich für den Zeitraum 1995 *bis* 1997, AMS, Wien.

Boyland, O. and G. Nicoletti (2001),
   "Regulatory Reform in Retail Distribution", *OECD Economic Studies* No. 32, 2001/I.

Breuss, F. and K. Steininger (1998),
   "Biomass Energy Use to Reduce Climate Change: A General Equilibrium Analysis for Austria", *Journal of Policy Modelling*, 20(4): 513-535.

Breuss, Fritz (2001),
   "Towards a political economy of zero budgeting in Austria", *Empirica* 28/1.

Bundesministerium für Arbeit, Gesundheit und Soziales (1999),
   Chancengleichheit von Frauen und Männern – Die Umsetzung des Arbeitsmarktpolitischen Zieles im europäischen Sozialfonds in Österreich, Wien.

Bundesministerium fur Umwelt, Jugend und Familie (1998),
   "Bioenergie-Cluster Österreich", Band 39/1998.

Bundesministerium für Wirtschaft und Arbeit (2000),
   Liberalisation of the Austrian Natural Gas Market, Wien.

Bundesministerium für Wissenschaft und Verkehr (1997),
   Einzel- und gesamtwirtschaftliche Wegekostenrechnung Strasse/Schiene in Österreich und der Schweiz,
   Wien.

Czerny, M, M. Pfaffermayr, G. Schwarz, R. Wieser (2001),
   "Konjunkturabschwächung in Europe Beeinträchtigt Investitionsbereitschaft der
   Unternehmen", WIFO Monatsberichte 8/2001.

ECB (2001),
   Price effects of regulatory reform in selected network industries.

ECMT (2000),
   Efficient transport taxes and charges, OECD, Paris.

EU Commission (2000a),
   Commission Recommendation – amending Commission Recommendation 98/511I/EC of 29 July 1998
   on Interconnection in a liberalised telecommunications market, Brussels.

EU Commission (2000b),
   Sixth report on the implementation of the telecommunications regulatory package, COM 2000(814),
   Brussels.

EU Commission (2000c),
   Proposal for a European Parliament and Council Directive – amending directive 97/67/EC with regard
   to the further opening to Competition of Community postal services, Brussels.

EU Commission (2001),
   Directive of the European Parliament and of the Council, amending Directives 96/92/EC and 92/30/EC
   concerning common rules for the internal market in electricity and natural gas, Brussels.

Evans, J., D. Lippoldt and P. Mariana (2001),
   "Trends in working hours in OECD countries", Social Policy Occasional Papers, No. 45, OECD,
   Paris.

Farmer, K. and K. W. Steininger (1999),
   "Reducing CO_2-emissions Under Fiscal Retrenchment: A Multi-Cohort CGE-Model for
   Austria", Environmental and Resource Economics, 13, p.309-340.

Fay, R. (1996),
   "Enhancing the effectiveness of active labour market policies: evidence from pro-
   gramme evaluations in OECD countries", Labour Market and Social Policy Occasional Papers
   No. 18, OECD, Paris.

Federal Ministry of Agriculture, Forestry, Environment and Water (2000),
   Federal Act on Environmental Impact Assessment (EIA Act 2000), Wien.

Federal Ministry of Environment, Youth and Family Affairs (1998),
   Federal Waste Management Plan 1998, Wien.

Fehr-Duda, Helga, Ferdinand Lechner, Peter Neudorfer, Walter Reiter and Andreas Riesenfelder (1996),
   Die Effektivität arbeitsmarktpolitischer Beschäftigungsmassnahmen in Österreich, AMS, Wien.

FGG (2000),
   Evaluierungsbericht – Ergebnisse und Schlussfolgerungen, Wien.

Fiedler, Franz (2001),
    Evaluierung von Ausgliederungen durch den Rechnungshof, mimeo, Wien.

Friedl, B. and K. Steininger (2001),
    "An Austrian Economic model for Environmentally Sustainable Transports", project paper financed by the Austrian Federal Ministry of Agriculture, Forestry, Environment and Water Management.

Guger, Alois and Christine Mayrhuber (2001),
    "Labour force participation and public pension system" in *Austrian Economic Quarterly* 2/2001, WIFO, Wien.

Hagen, Tobias, and Viktor Steiner (2000),
    Von der Finanzierung der Arbeitslosigkeit zur Förderung von Arbeit, Baden-Baden.

Hofer, Helmut and Reinhard Koman (2001),
    Social security and retirement in Austria, Institute for Advanced Studies, Research report July/2001, Wien.

Huber, Peter and Ewald Walterskirchen (1999),
    Möglichkeiten einer regionalen Arbeitsmarktpolitik in Oberösterreich, WIFO, Wien.

IEA (1998),
    Energy Policies of IEA Countries – Austria 1998 Review, Paris.

Joumard, I. (2001),
    "Tax Systems in European Union Countries", *Economics Department Working Paper No. 301*, OECD, Paris.

Kerschner, F. and B. Binder (1998),
    "Neues Verkersrecht als Instrument des Umweltschutzes", Studie im Auftrag des Bundesministeriums für Umwelt, Jugend und Familie.

Kletzan, D. (2000),
    Klimarelevanz des österreicheischen Forderungssystems, WIFO.

Kletzan, D. and A. Köppl (2001),
    "CO_2 emissions trading – an instrument for the Austrian climate strategy", *Austrian Economic Quarterly* 1/2001.

Koeppl, A, K. Kratena, C. Pichl, F. Schebeck, S. Schleicher and M. Wueger (1996),
    "Macroeconomic and Sectoral Effects of Energy Taxation in Austria", *Environmental and Resource Economics*, 8.

Kommunal Kredit (1999),
    Annual Report.

Kosz, M. (1996),
    "Valuing riverside wetlands: the case of the Donau-Auen' national park", *Ecological Economics* 16.

Kropf, Katharina, Heinz Leitsmüller and Bruno Rossmann (2001),
    Ausgliederungen aus dem öffentlichen Bereich, Wien.

Lassnigg, Lorenz and Mario Steiner (2000),
    Evaluierung der stiftungsähnlichen Massnahme DYNAMO für Langzeitarbeitslose, AMS, Wien.

Lassnigg, Lorenz, Andrea Leitner, Peter Steiner and Angela Wrobleweski (1999),
    Unterstützung beim Wiedereinstieg – Möglichkeiten und Wirkungen frauenspezifischer Massnahmen, AMS, Wien.

Lechner, Ferdinand, Rainer Loidl, Lukas Mitterauer, Walter Reiter and Andreas Riesenfelder (2000),
   Aktive Arbeitsmarktpolitik im Brennpunkt I: Evaluierung sozialökonomischer Betriebe, AMS, Wien.

Lechner, Ferdinand, Walter Reiter and Andreas Riesenfelder (2000),
   Anforderungsgerecht – Ergebnis der Evaluierung des Beschäftigungsprogrammes "Aktion 8000", AMS, Wien.

Lehner, Gerhard (2001),
   "Finanzausgleich als Instrument der Budgetpolitik", WIFO *Monatsberichte*, 8/2001.

Leibfritz, Willi, John Thornton and Alexandra Bibbee (1997),
   "Taxation and economic performance", *Economics Department Working Paper No. 176*, OECD, Paris.

Martin, J. (1998),
   "What works among active labour market policies: evidence from OECD countries'experience", OECD *Economic Studies No. 30*, Paris.

Mayrhuber, Christine (2000),
   "Umstellung des Abfertigungsrechts: Impuls oder Hemmnis auf dem österreichischen Arbeitsmarkt?", WIFO *Monatsbericht No. 12/2000*.

Ministry of Economic Affairs and Labour (2001),
   Full Liberalisation of the Austrian Electricity Market, Wien.

Ministry of Economic Affairs and Labour (2001),
   Structural reforms of product and capital markets – Austria 2000, the third national progress report as specified in the conclusions of the Cardiff European Council of June 1998, Wien.

Mitterauer, Lukas, Walter Reiter and Andreas Riesenfelder (1999),
   Endbericht, Evaluation der BESEB 1997, Arbeitsmarktservice Österreich, mimeo, Wien.

O'Brien, P. and A. Vourc'h (2001),
   "Encouraging Environmentally Sustainable Growth: Experience in OECD Countries", *Economics Department Working Papers No. 293*, OECD, Paris.

OECD (1994),
   The OECD Jobs Study, Facts, Analysis, Strategies, Paris.

OECD (1995),
   Environmental Performance Review of Austria, Paris.

OECD (1996), *Economic Survey of Austria*, Paris.

OECD (1997),
   Economic Survey of Austria, Paris.

OECD (1998a),
   Economic Survey of Austria, Paris.

OECD (1998b),
   "Indicators for the Integration of Environmental Concerns into Transport Policies".

OECD (1999a),
   Economic Survey of Austria, Paris.

OECD (1999b),
   Economic Survey of Germany, Paris.

OECD (1999c),
   Regulatory Reform in the United States, Paris.

OECD (1999*d*),
"Relationships Between Regulators and Competition Authorities", *Series Roundtables on Competition Policy*, No. 22, Paris.

OECD (1999*e*),
Economic Survey of Sweden, Paris.

OECD (1999*f*),
"Promoting Competition in Postal Services", *Series Roundtables on Competition Policy*, No. 24, Paris.

OECD (1999*g*),
National Climate Policies and the Kyoto Protocol, Paris.

OECD (1999*h*),
Action Against Climate Change: The Kyoto Protocol and Beyond, Paris.

OECD (1999*i*),
The Price of Water, Paris.

OECD (1999*j*),
Implementing Domestic Tradable Permits for Environmental Protection, Paris.

OECD (2000*a*),
Employment Outlook, Paris.

OECD (2000*b*),
Economic Survey of the United States, Paris.

OECD (2000*c*),
Economic Survey of Denmark, Paris.

OECD (2001*a*),
"Fiscal Implications of Age-related Spending" in OECD *Economic Outlook* 69, Paris.

OECD (2001*b*),
Employment Outlook, Paris.

OECD (2001*c*),
Labour Market Policies and the Public Employment Service, Paris.

OECD (2001*d*),
Innovations in Labour Market Policies: the Australian way, Paris.

OECD (2001*e*),
Economic Survey of Australia, Paris.

OECD (2001*f*),
Economic Survey of Germany, Paris.

OECD (2001*g*),
Education at a Glance, Paris.

OECD (2001*h*),
Regulatory Review of the United Kingdom, (forthcoming).

OECD (2001*i*),
"Report on leniency programmes to fight hard core cartels", OECD *Journal of Competition Law and Policy*, Vol. 3, No. 3, Paris.

OECD (2001*j*),
"Structural separation in regulated industries" in *Restructuring Public Utilities for Competition*, Paris.

OECD (2001k),
Communication Outlook, Paris.

OECD (2001l),
"Competition Issues in Telecommunications", Series Round tables on Competition, forthcoming Paris.

OECD (2001m),
The Development of Broadband Access in OECD countries, Paris.

OECD (2001n),
Economic Survey of Belgium, Paris.

OECD (2001o),
Economic Outlook No. 69, June, Paris.

OECD (2001p),
Domestic Transferable Permits for Environmental Management – Design and Implementation, Paris.

Österreichisches Institut für Wirtschaftsforschung, Institut für höhere Studien (2000),
Begleitende Bewertung der Umsetzung des nationalen Aktionsplanes für Beschäftigung im Jahr 1999, Wien.

Pearce, Davis (1998),
"Cost benefit analysis and environmental policy", Oxford Review of Economic Policy, Vol. 14, No. 4, 1998, and articles therein.

Pichl C., W. Puwein, I. Obernberger, H. Voraberger, K. Steininger (1998),
"Erneuerbare Energieträger in Österreichs Wirtschaft", WIFO.

Pollan, Wolfgang (2001),
"Lohndrift und Lohnunterschiede in der Industrie seit 1981", WIFO, Monatsberichte No. 3.

Puwein, W. (1996),
"Das Problem des Tanktourismus" WIFO Monatsberichte 11/1996.

Puwein, Wilfried (1998),
"The Transit Agreement: A Preliminary Assessment", Austrian Economic Quarterly, 2/1998.

Puwein, W. (1999),
"Investitionen in die Bahn- und Strasseninfrastruktur", WIFO Monatsberichte 8/1999.

Puwein, W. (2001),
"Effects of EU Enlargement on Transport in Austria", WIFO Monatsberichte No. 8.

Riggs, Leslie (2001),
"Introduction of contestability in the delivery of employment services in Australia" in OECD (2001),
Labour market policies and the public employment service, Paris.

Rudolph, K.-U. (1998),
"European Comparison of Sewerage Charges", Research project No. 30/96 for the Federal Ministry of the Economic Affairs and the Federal Ministry for the Environment, Nature Conservation and Nuclear Safety, Berlin.

Schleicher, S., K. Kratena and K. Radunsky (1999),
Die österreichische CO_2-Bilanz 1997 – Struktur und Dynamik der österreichischen CO_2-Emissionen, Austrian Council on Climate Change.

Sinabell, F. (2001),
"Empirical work on multi-functionality – Report on Austria", unpublished OECD paper.

Stagl, S. (2001),
  "Local Organic Food Markets – Potentials and limitations for contributing to sustainable development", paper presented at the 2001 Annual meeting of the Austrian Economic Society in Graz.

Steiner, F. (2001),
  "Regulation, Industry Structure and Performance in the Electricity Supply Industry", OECD *Economic Studies* No. 32, 2001/I.

Van den Noord, Paul and Christopher Heady (2001),
  Surveillance of tax policies: a synthesis of findings in economic surveys, *Economics Department Working Paper No .303*, OECD, Paris.

Walterskirchen, Ewald and Gudrun Biffl (2001),
  Knappheit an Arbeitskräften- Studie des Österreichischen Instituts für Wirtschaftsforschung im Auftrag der Wirtschaftskammer Österreich, Wien.

Walther, H. (1999),
  "Ökonomische Funktion der österreichischen Abfertigungsregelung", *Lichte der Theorie und Empirie*, Wirtschaftsuniversität Wien, mimeo.

Winter-Ebmer, R. (1998),
  "Potential unemployment benefit duration and spell length" lessons from a quasi experiment in Austria, Oxford Bulletin of Economics and Statistics 60.

Wirl, F. and G. Infanger (1985),
  "The Prospects of Energy Conservation: A Different Approach to the Fuel Demand for Space Heating", Empirica, Vol. 12, No. 5.

Zhuravskaya, Ekaterina V. (2001),
  "Incentives to Provide Local Public Goods: Fiscal Federalism, Russian Style", *Journal of Public Economics*, Vol. 76, No. 3.

Annex I

Chronology of main economic events

1999

March

The government presents a tax reform proposal to take effect from 1 January 2000. The main components include: a general lowering of marginal tax rates, larger tax allowances for R&D expenses and pension savings.

May

The spring wage negotiations lead to increases in collectively negotiated wages of between 1.9 per cent and 2.8 per cent.

October

General elections.

November

In a cooperation with Deutsche Börse AG, Wiener Börse joins the international electronic trading system Xetra for stock and bond trading, giving all market participants irrespective of their location access to electronic securities trading across borders.

Wage negotiations in the areas not settled in the spring lead to increases in collectively negotiated wages of between 2.0 per cent and 2.4 per cent.

2000

January

Legislation comes into force to induce higher part-time employment among older workers by providing financial support to working time reductions for older employees by subsidising compensation of those claiming part-time work (Altersteilzeit).

The tax reform 2000 and the second phase of the family benefits package come into force. They lower the tax burden on wage and other personal incomes, raise child benefits, and foster the attractiveness of Austria as a business location.

February

A new coalition government between the Austrian Peoples Party and the Freedom Party is formed.

March

The new government's first budget proposal for 2000 is presented, envisaging a general government deficit of 2 per cent of GDP. The proposal includes higher revenues from indirect taxes and a number of one-off measures. The 2000 budget comes into force in June 2000, and until then a provisional budget – based on the estimates of 1999 – remains in force.

May

The spring wage negotiations lead to increases in collectively negotiated wages of between 1.9 per cent and 2.8 per cent.

June

The following indirect taxes were increased: tobacco tax, levy on electricity, vehicle insurance tax as well as certain fees (e.g. for passports and other official documents).

The "Getränkesteuer" tax on beverages served in public premises is abolished to comply with an earlier ruling by the European Court of Justice and is replaced by increases in other indirect taxes, mainly on beverages, effective from 1 June 2000 and 1 January 2001.

The Austrian Banking Act is amended so as to reflect the abolition of anonymous savings accounts (effective from November 2000 onwards).

July

The energy liberalisation act passes Parliament, envisaging the full opening of the electricity and gas markets by October 2001 and October 2002, respectively.

September

The government proposes a two-year budget, targeting a halving of the general government deficit to 0.75 per cent of GDP in 2001 and a zero deficit in 2002 through a fiscal consolidation package. In addition, a further family support scheme is presented, to take effect in January 2002, making child support more generous and independent from previous employment.

October

The stock exchange turnover tax is abolished.

Wages in the federal government sector are set to increase by Sch 500/month in 2001 and 0.8 per cent the year after. Over the same horizon, federal government employment is to be reduced by 11 000 full time equivalents.

The Federal Government, the Länder and the local municipalities agree on a new revenue sharing arrangement (Finanzausgleich), to be in force up to 2004 as well as a pact on the joint achievement of the 2002 general government deficit target. The pact stipulates that the Länder are obliged to achieve budget surpluses, while local municipalities are required to balance their budgets. Non-compliance with these targets can lead to financial sanctions.

Pension reform measures come into effect, mainly designed to raise retirement ages.

November

The NEWEX (New Europe Exchange) opens for stock exchange trading and is specialised in Central and Eastern European securities. The new exchange is a joint venture of Deutsche Börse AG and Wiener Börse AG.

The auction of UMTS licenses results in revenue of nearly Sch 11 ½ billion (€ 835 million) with the licenses allocated to 6 companies, each receiving two set of frequencies.

The privatisation of the Postal Savings Bank is completed. Further sales of shares in Telekom Austria and the Vienna airport takes place, lowering the government owned share to 47.8 per cent and 8.9 per cent, respectively.

The wage negotiations in the areas that were not settled in the spring leads to increases in collectively negotiated wages of between 2.5 per cent and 3.7 per cent.

December

Parliament passes the 2001 budget.

2001

January

The unemployment benefit insurance system is reformed.

The Hospital and Major Equipment Plan comes into force, introducing elements of enhanced nation-wide co-ordination in the planning of hospital supply.

March

The government commissioned Task Reform Commission – part of the ongoing administrative reform in the public sector – publishes a list of proposals for out-sourcing government services to private providers and for streamlining government services.

April

The 2002 budget is legislated.

May

The federal government's ownership in the postal and telecommunication sectors is transferred to the public sector industrial holding company (ÖIAG). The continuation of the privatisation programme leads to the sale of an additional 30 per cent of *Austria Telekom* and all shares in *Austria Tabak*.

The spring wage negotiations lead to increases in collectively negotiated wages of between 2.6 per cent and 3.1 per cent.

June

The government presents its proposal for reform of the Austrian Competition Law, which introduces an independent Federal Competition Authority and a Cartel Prosecutor. Parliament passed a law to unify financial market supervision, to come into force on 1 April 2002.

July

Parliament passes the act on child cash support (Kinderbetreuungsgeld), thereby extending family benefits, which will come into force January 1, 2002.

October

The introduction of a tuition fee for university students takes effect with the beginning of the winter semester 2001/02; its proceeds will partly be distributed to the universities for investment purposes.

As part of the ongoing administrative reform process, government presents a bill on public sector reform (Verwaltungsreformgesetz 2001).

BASIC STATISTICS:

INTERNATIONAL COMPARISONS

	Units	Reference period[1]	Australia	Austria
Population				
Total ....Thousands	Thousands	1998	18 730	8 078
Inhabitants per sq. km ....Number	Number	1998	2	96
Net average annual increase over previous 10 years..............%	%	1998	1.3	0.6
Employment				
Total civilian employment (TCE)[2] ....Thousands	Thousands	1998	8 596	3 689
of which:				
Agriculture...% of TCE	% of TCE	1998	4.8	6.6
Industry...% of TCE	% of TCE	1998	21.9	31.8
Services...% of TCE	% of TCE	1998	73.3	61.7
Gross domestic product (GDP)				
At current prices and current exchange rates ....Bill. US$	Bill. US$	1998	372.7	210.9
Per capita ....US$	US$	1998	19 899	26 108
At current prices using current PPPs[3] ....Bill. US$	Bill. US$	1998	440.0	193.1
Per capita ....US$	US$	1998	23 492	23 900
Average annual volume growth over previous 5 years.............%	%	1998	4.4	2.2
Gross fixed capital formation (GFCF) ....% of GDP	% of GDP	1998	23.8	23.5
of which:				
Machinery and equipment ....% of GDP	% of GDP	1998	10.3 (96)	9.3
Residential construction ....% of GDP	% of GDP	1998	4.4 (96)	6.4
Average annual volume growth over previous 5 years.............%	%	1998	2.7	0.2
Gross saving ratio[4] ....% of GDP	% of GDP	1998	20.1	22.6
General government				
Current expenditure on goods and services ....% of GDP	% of GDP	1998	18.2	19.8
Current disbursements[5] ....% of GDP	% of GDP	1998	32.0	47.8
Current receipts[6]	% of GDP	1998	33.3	47.7
Net official development assistance ....% of GNP	% of GNP	1998	0.27	0.22
Indicators of living standards				
Private consumption per capita using current PPPs[3] ....US$	US$	1998	14 379	13 417
Passengers cars, per 1 000 inhabitants.........................Number	Number	1998	630	481
Internet hosts, per 1 000 inhabitants[7].........................Number	Number	1999	55	28
Television sets, per 1 000 inhabitants ....Number	Number	1998	495 (95)	331
Doctors, per 1 000 inhabitants................................Number	Number	1998	2.6	2.0
Infant mortality per 1 000 live births..........................Number	Number	1998	5.8 (96)	6.6
Wages and prices (average annual increase rate over previous 5 years)..				
Wages (earnings or rates according to availability) ....%	%	1998	1.9	3.3
Consumer prices ....%	%	1998	2.0	1.8
Foreign trade[8]				
Exports of goods, fob ....Mill. US$	Mill. US$	1998	55 885	62 742
As % of GDP...%	%	1998	12.7	32.5
Average annual increase rate over previous 5 years ....%	%	1998	5.7	9.3
Imports of goods, cif.......................................Mill. US$	Mill. US$	1998	60 821	68 183
As % of GDP...%	%	1998	13.8	35.3
Average annual increase rate over previous 5 years ....%	%	1998	7.5	7.0
Total official reserves[9] ....Mill. SDR's	Mill. SDR's	1998	10 942	22 324
As ratio of average monthly imports of goods...................Ratio	Ratio	1998	2.2	4.3

1. Unless otherwise stated.
2. According to the definitions used in OECD *Labour Force Statistics.*
3. PPPs = Purchasing Power Parities.
4. Gross Saving = Gross national disposable income minus private and government consumption.

EMPLOYMENT OPPORTUNITIES
Economics Department, OECD

The Economics Department of the OECD offers challenging and rewarding opportunities to economists interested in applied policy analysis in an international environment. The Department's concerns extend across the entire field of economic policy analysis, both macro-economic and microeconomic. Its main task is to provide, for discussion by committees of senior officials from Member countries, documents and papers dealing with current policy concerns. Within this programme of work, three major responsibilities are:

- to prepare regular surveys of the economies of individual Member countries;
- to issue full twice-yearly reviews of the economic situation and prospects of the OECD countries in the context of world economic trends;
- to analyse specific policy issues in a medium-term context for the OECD as a whole, and to a lesser extent for the non-OECD countries.

The documents prepared for these purposes, together with much of the Department's other economic work, appear in published form in the *OECD Economic Outlook, OECD Economic Surveys, OECD Economic Studies* and the Department's *Working Papers* series.

The Department maintains a world econometric model, INTERLINK, which plays an important role in the preparation of the policy analyses and twice-yearly projections. The availability of extensive cross-country data bases and good computer resources facilitates comparative empirical analysis, much of which is incorporated into the model.

The Department is made up of about 80 professional economists from a variety of backgrounds and Member countries. Most projects are carried out by small teams and last from four to eighteen months. Within the Department, ideas and points of view are widely discussed; there is a lively professional interchange, and all professional staff have the opportunity to contribute actively to the programme of work.

Skills the Economics Department is looking for:

a) Solid competence in using the tools of both microeconomic and macroeconomic theory to answer policy questions. Experience indicates that this normally requires the equivalent of a Ph.D. in economics or substantial relevant professional experience to compensate for a lower degree.

b) Solid knowledge of economic statistics and quantitative methods; this includes how to identify data, estimate structural relationships, apply basic techniques of time series analysis, and test hypotheses. It is essential to be able to interpret results sensibly in an economic policy context.

c) A keen interest in and extensive knowledge of policy issues, economic developments and their political/social contexts.

d) Interest and experience in analysing questions posed by policy-makers and presenting the results to them effectively and judiciously. Thus, work experience in government agencies or policy research institutions is an advantage.

e) The ability to write clearly, effectively, and to the point. The OECD is a bilingual organisation with French and English as the official languages. Candidates must have excellent knowledge of one of these languages, and some knowledge of the other. Knowledge of other languages might also be an advantage for certain posts.

f) For some posts, expertise in a particular area may be important, but a successful candidate is expected to be able to work on a broader range of topics relevant to the work of the Department. Thus, except in rare cases, the Department does not recruit narrow specialists.

g) The Department works on a tight time schedule with strict deadlines. Moreover, much of the work in the Department is carried out in small groups. Thus, the ability to work with other economists from a variety of cultural and professional backgrounds, to supervise junior staff, and to produce work on time is important.

General information

The salary for recruits depends on educational and professional background. Positions carry a basic salary from FF 318 660 or FF 393 192 for Administrators (economists) and from FF 456 924 for Principal Administrators (senior economists). This may be supplemented by expatriation and/or family allowances, depending on nationality, residence and family situation. Initial appointments are for a fixed term of two to three years.

Vacancies are open to candidates from OECD Member countries. The Organisation seeks to maintain an appropriate balance between female and male staff and among nationals from Member countries.

For further information on employment opportunities in the Economics Department, contact:

Management Support Unit
Economics Department
OECD
2, rue André-Pascal
75775 PARIS CEDEX 16
FRANCE

E-Mail: eco.contact@oecd.org

Applications citing ''ECSUR'', together with a detailed *curriculum vitae* in English or French, should be sent to the Head of Personnel at the above address.

OECD PUBLICATIONS, 2, rue André-Pascal, 75775 PARIS CEDEX 16
PRINTED IN FRANCE
(10 2001 11 1 P) ISBN 92-64-19669-2 – No. 52199 2001
ISSN 0376-6438